YOUR FUTURE
YOUR WAY

JOBS AND CAREERS FOR TEENAGERS

(CAREER BOOK FOR TEENS)

Hannah P Cartwright

© **Copyright 2026 - All rights reserved.**

The content contained within this book may not be reproduced, duplicated or transmitted without direct written permission from the author or the publisher.

Under no circumstances will any blame or legal responsibility be held against the publisher, or author, for any damages, reparation, or monetary loss due to the information contained within this book, either directly or indirectly.

Legal Notice:

This book is copyright protected. It is only for personal use. You cannot amend, distribute, sell, use, quote or paraphrase any part, or the content within this book, without the consent of the author or publisher.

Disclaimer Notice:

Please note the information contained within this document is for educational and entertainment purposes only. All effort has been executed to present accurate, up to date, reliable, complete information. No warranties of any kind are declared or implied. Readers acknowledge that the author is not engaged in the rendering of legal, financial, medical or professional advice. The content within this book has been derived from various sources. Please consult a licensed professional before attempting any techniques outlined in this book.

By reading this document, the reader agrees that under no circumstances is the author responsible for any losses, direct or indirect, that are incurred as a result of the use of the information contained within this document, including, but not limited to, errors, omissions, or inaccuracies.

This book is an original publication by the author and is not licensed, resold, or distributed as PLR, Creative Commons, or master resell content.

Published by CB Storyworks.

First Edition

ISBN 978-1-7645449-0-0 (eBook)

ISBN 978-1-7644668-9-9 (Paperback)

About the Author
Hannah P Cartwright

Hannah isn't just another writer—she's your go-to guide for navigating life's ups and downs. Her book, *Your Future, Your Way: Jobs and Careers for Teenagers (Career Book for Teens)*, is a practical toolkit that equips you with the necessary tools to overcome challenges and build an exciting future.

With a deep passion for personal growth, Hannah combines real-life coaching experience with solid research to provide practical strategies. She is honest and offers advice that feels like a pep talk from a mentor who understands your journey—no sugar-coating, just straight-up, practical tips to help you thrive.

Hannah, a Personal Development Guide, Wellness Advisor, Mentor, and Mom, knows how to connect deeply. Her books aren't just pages filled with words—they're your toolkit for success, crafted from her experiences and understanding of teenagers' challenges.

If you're ready to level up, tap into your potential, and start building your desired future, Hannah P. Cartwright is here to help. Let's get started!

Abstract

Welcome to your journey of career discovery! This guide is designed to help you navigate the exciting but sometimes overwhelming process of finding your perfect career path. We'll explore traditional and emerging careers, discuss how to align your passions with practical opportunities and provide concrete strategies for building your future. Whether you're a freshman just starting to think about careers or a senior planning your next steps, this book will help you understand the modern job landscape, develop essential skills, and create a personalized roadmap to success. Together, we'll explore how to balance your dreams with reality, leverage technology and AI, and build a fulfilling career that evolves with you.

Contents

Introduction   1

1. Your Career DNA   3
    Understanding Your Unique Strengths and Passions (Ikigai)
       Discovering Your Natural Talents: Assessment Tools and Self-Reflection
       Understanding Ikigai: Where Passion Meets Purpose
       Mapping Your Career DNA: Creating Your Personal Strength Profile

2. Modern Career Landscape   13
    Exploring Traditional, Digital, and Emerging Opportunities
       Evolution of Traditional Careers in the Digital Age
       Emerging Digital Careers and Remote Work Opportunities
       Future-Proofing Your Career: Essential Skills for Tomorrow's Jobs

3. The Smart Path Forward   22
    College, Trade School, or Alternative Routes?
       Understanding the ROI: Comparing Costs and Benefits of Different Educational Paths
       Trade Schools and Apprenticeships: Skills-Based Career Development

Alternative Routes: Entrepreneurship, Certifications, and Self-Directed Learning

4. Digital Success   34

Leveraging AI and Technology for Your Own Business

    Understanding AI Tools: From Chatbots to Content Creation

    Digital Business Models: Identifying Your Online Niche

    Building Your Digital Presence: Social Media Strategy and Online Marketing

    Key Takeaways

Leave A Review   43

Thank You!

5. Building Your Experience Bank   44

Real-World Skills and International Experience That Matter

    Strategic Volunteering and Internships: Building Professional Experience While in School

    Global Perspective: Exchange Programs, Virtual International Experiences, and Cultural Competency

    Documenting Your Journey: Creating a Professional Portfolio and Experience Log

    Key Takeaways

6. Money Smart   55

Funding Your Future Without the Stress

    Smart Education Funding: Scholarships, Grants, and Loan Navigation

    Building Your Financial Foundation: Budgeting and Saving Strategies

Understanding Credit and Making Smart Money Choices

7. The Multi-Passionate Path   65
   Creating Your Portfolio Career
   - Building Multiple Income Streams: Combining Part-time Work, Freelancing, and Side Hustles
   - Time Management and Work-Life Integration for Multi-Passionate Professionals
   - Creating a Unified Personal Brand Across Different Professional Roles
   - Key Takeaway

8. Building Your Brand   74
   Networking and Personal Marketing in the Digital Age
   - Digital Presence Management: Creating and Maintaining Your Professional Online Identity
   - Strategic Networking: Building Authentic Professional Relationships Online and Offline
   - Personal Marketing Tools: From LinkedIn Profiles to Digital Portfolios
   - Key Takeaways

9. Family Dynamics   85
   Navigating Career Conversations with Parents and Overcoming Self-Doubt
   - Effective Communication Strategies: Having Productive Career Discussions with Parents
   - Managing Cultural and Generational Expectations in Career Choices

      Building Self-Confidence: Overcoming Career-Related Self-Doubt and Imposter Syndrome

10. Your Success Blueprint   95

    Creating a Flexible Career Strategy

      Strategic Planning: Creating Your Five-Year Flexible Career Map

      Identifying Pivot Points: Building Career Adaptability and Backup Plans

      Goal Setting and Milestone Creation: From Vision to Action Steps

      Key Takeaways

Conclusion   106

Bibliography   108

Introduction

Do you ever feel overwhelmed when thinking about your future career? Trust me, you're not alone. As a career guide working with countless teenagers, I've seen firsthand how daunting it can be to navigate the maze of career choices, especially when it seems like everyone has an opinion about what you "should" do with your life. That's precisely why I wrote this book - to be your companion on this exciting journey of discovering your unique career path.

The world of work is changing faster than ever before. Traditional career paths are being transformed by technology, new opportunities are emerging daily, and the idea of having a single lifetime career is becoming as outdated as a flip phone. But here's the exciting part - this rapid change means there have never been more possibilities for you to create a career that truly fits who you are.

In this book, we'll explore everything from understanding your personal Career DNA to leveraging artificial intelligence for your own business ventures. We'll look at traditional paths like college and trade schools and dive into alternative routes that might better suit your goals. Whether you're passionate about technology, dream of starting your own business, or aren't quite sure what interests you yet, you'll find practical guidance and fundamental strategies you can use right now.

Through my years of experience coaching teens, I've noticed that many career guides focus only on the "what" of career choices, listing endless job titles and requirements. But what you really need is the "how" - how to discover what truly excites you, gain real experience while still in school, talk to your parents about your career choices, and fund your dreams without drowning in debt. That's precisely what we'll cover in these pages.

You'll meet teens like Sarah, who combined her love of art with medicine to become a medical illustrator, and Alex, who modernized his family's traditional bookstore using social media marketing. Their stories and many others will show you how thinking creatively about your career can open up possibilities you might never have imagined.

This isn't just another book telling you what to do with your life. Instead, think of it as your personal career toolkit, filled with practical strategies, real-world examples, and actionable steps you can take right now. Whether you're 14 and just starting to think about your future or 19 and already on your career journey, you'll find valuable insights and guidance here.

Remember, your career path doesn't have to look like anyone else's. In fact, the most fulfilling careers often don't follow a straight line. As you read through these chapters, you'll discover how to create your own unique path - one that combines your interests, talents, and values in a way that's genuinely yours.

So, are you ready to start building your future your way? Let's begin this journey together, exploring the exciting possibilities that await you in the modern world of work. Whether you have a clear vision of your dream career or are just starting to explore your options, this book will help you navigate your path confidently and purposefully.

Your future is waiting, and it's full of possibilities. Let's discover them together.

Chapter 1

Your Career DNA

Understanding Your Unique Strengths and Passions (Ikigai)

Have you ever wondered why some people seem to know exactly what they want to do with their lives while others struggle to find their direction? Just like your biological DNA makes you unique, your Career DNA - the distinctive blend of your talents, passions, and values - holds the key to finding a fulfilling career path. This unique combination isn't just some random mix - it's the foundation for finding work that truly lights you up. Think of it as your personal compass guiding you toward opportunities that feel right for *you*, not just what everyone else thinks you should do.

I see this journey of self-discovery play out regularly in my career guidance workshops. One story that really stands out is about Sarah, a sixteen-year-old student who came to me feeling totally stressed about choosing between her artistic passion and her parents' dreams of becoming a doctor. The pressure was real, and I could see her torn between these seemingly opposite paths.

We started mapping out Sarah's Career DNA using the Ikigai framework (a Japanese concept that helps you find where your purpose and happiness intersect). As we dug deeper into her interests and talents, something fascinating emerged. Her artistic abilities weren't just about creating pretty pictures - she had this incredible knack for taking complex information and turning it into clear, visual explanations that anyone could understand.

This revelation opened up a whole new world of possibilities. Instead of choosing between art *or* medicine, Sarah discovered the field of medical illustration - a perfect blend of both worlds. Today, she studies biomedical visualization, creating detailed medical artwork that helps doctors and patients better understand complex medical concepts. She found a way to honor both her creative talents *and* her interest in healthcare.

Your own journey of discovering your Career DNA might feel overwhelming right now, and that's totally normal. Maybe you're feeling pressured to "figure it all out" or worried about making the "wrong" choice. But here's the thing - understanding your Career DNA isn't about limiting yourself or picking just one path. It's about discovering all the unique ways your different interests and talents can work together.

This chapter will explore practical tools and exercises to help you map out your Career DNA. You'll learn how to identify your natural talents (yes, everyone has them!), develop your interests into marketable skills, and understand how your values can guide your career choices. We'll look at how to use the Ikigai framework to find that sweet spot where what you love doing meets what the world needs.

Through real stories and practical examples, you'll see how other teens have navigated this journey of self-discovery. More importantly, you'll learn that finding your path isn't about making one big decision - it's about taking small steps to understand yourself better and keeping an open mind to possibilities you might not have considered yet.

Discovering Your Natural Talents: Assessment Tools and Self-Reflection

Ever catch yourself doing something so naturally that you barely have to think about it while your friends struggle with the same task? That's a clue to your natural talents - those unique abilities that feel right when you use them. But here's the thing: sometimes, our talents are so natural to us that we don't even realize they're special. It's like being a fish who doesn't know it's fantastic at swimming because that's just what it does!

Let's break down some practical ways to uncover your natural talents. First up are self-reflection exercises - think of these as your personal talent detective tools. Try keeping a "wins journal" for a week, jotting down moments when you feel energized and successful or lose track of time because you're so absorbed in what you're doing. Maybe you notice you always end up organizing group projects (hello, leadership skills!) or friends constantly ask for your help to explain complicated topics (teaching ability alert!).

One of my favorite exercises for teens is the "Compliment Collection." Here's how it works: for one week, write down every genuine compliment you received and what you did when you got it. You might notice patterns - like always being praised for how you explain things, solve problems, or make others feel heard. These patterns are golden clues to your natural talents.

But don't just rely on self-reflection - there are tons of free online assessment tools that can help you understand your strengths better. Websites like 16Personalities offer free personality assessments that can give insights into your natural working style and potential career fits. The VIA Character Strengths Survey is another free tool that helps identify your core strengths - and it's specifically designed to be teen-friendly.

Look for activities where you:

- Lose track of time while doing them
- Feel energized rather than drained
- Learn quickly and naturally
- Receive consistent positive feedback
- Find yourself helping others

I remember working with Miguel, a quiet sophomore who was convinced he didn't have any unique talents because he wasn't a star athlete or top of his class academically. Through our talent discovery exercises, he realized that his ability to calm down angry friends and help them see different perspectives wasn't just "being nice" - it was a valuable talent for conflict resolution and mediation. Today, he works toward becoming a peer counselor at his school, using his natural talent to make a real difference.

Another powerful way to uncover your talents is through what I call the "Energy Audit." Pay attention to which activities energize you and which drain you. For instance, do you feel pumped up after helping someone solve a tech problem? That might signal a natural talent for technical troubleshooting. Does organizing your notes into color-coded systems make you feel satisfied while others find it tedious? That could point to natural organizational abilities.

Questions to ask yourself during self-reflection:

- What do people often ask for my help with?
- Which subjects or activities do I pick up quickly?
- What kinds of problems do I enjoy solving?
- When do I feel most confident?
- What do trusted friends and family say I'm good at?

Remember, talents aren't just about academic or athletic abilities. Maybe you're great at spotting trends on social media, creating engaging video content, or helping people feel comfortable in group settings. These are all valuable talents in today's world. The key is to look beyond traditional definitions of talent and recognize that your unique combination of abilities makes you special.

As you explore your talents, keep a growth mindset. Natural talents are just the starting point - they're like seeds that need nurturing to grow into real strengths. Once you identify a talent, look for opportunities to develop it further through practice, learning, and real-world application. Join clubs, volunteer, take online courses, or start small projects that let you exercise these abilities.

The most important thing to remember is that everyone has natural talents - absolutely everyone, including you! Sometimes, they're obvious, like being great at public speaking, and sometimes, they're subtle, like having a knack for explaining complicated ideas in simple ways. Your job isn't to create talents from scratch but to discover and develop the unique abilities you already have.

Understanding Ikigai: Where Passion Meets Purpose

Have you ever heard of Ikigai? This super cool Japanese concept is like a roadmap for finding work you'll love doing.

Think of it as finding your sweet spot where four important things overlap:

- What you're good at
- What you love doing
- What the world needs
- What you can get paid for

Pretty neat, right?

When I explain Ikigai to teens in my workshops, I often use the example of playing video games. Let's say you're terrific at gaming (that's your skill), and you absolutely love it (there's your passion).

But how does that translate into a career?

Well, maybe you could become a game tester (something you can be paid for) or create tutorials helping others learn to play better (something the world needs). The magic happens when you find ways to combine all these elements.

Let's break down the four elements of Ikigai in a way that makes sense for your career planning:

- What you love (your passion)
- What you're good at (your talent)
- What the world needs (market demand)
- What you can be paid for (economic value)

One of my favorite success stories is about a student named Tyler who came to my workshop feeling totally lost about his future. He loved creating TikTok videos (his passion) and was really good at explaining things to others (his talent). We discovered that businesses needed help reaching younger audiences (market demand) and were willing to pay for social media expertise (economic value). Today, Tyler runs a successful social media consultancy while still in high school, helping local businesses connect with teen customers.

But here's the thing about Ikigai - it's not about finding the perfect overlap immediately. It's more like a journey of discovery. Maybe you only have two or three elements figured out right now, and that's totally okay! The key is to start somewhere and keep exploring until you find that sweet spot.

Here are some questions to help you explore each element of your own Ikigai:

- What activities make you lose track of time?
- Which skills come naturally to you?
- What problems do you see in your community or world that you'd like to solve?
- What services or skills do people seem willing to pay for?

Think of Ikigai as a puzzle where you're trying to fit together different pieces of yourself. Sometimes, you might need to reshape or find new pieces until everything clicks. And unlike a regular puzzle, there's no single "right" way for it to look at the end.

One common misconception I hear from teens is that they need to have it all figured out right now. That's not how Ikigai works! Your sweet spot might shift as you grow, learn new skills, and discover new interests—and that's perfectly normal. The goal isn't to find one perfect career for the rest of your life but to understand how to align your work with what matters to you.

Here's a practical exercise I use with my students: Create four lists, one for each element of Ikigai. Under "What you love," write down everything you enjoy doing, no matter how random it seems. Under "What you're good at," list your skills and talents. For "What the world needs," research current problems or challenges that interest you. Finally, under "What you can be paid for," look up careers or services related to your interests and skills.

Look for patterns and connections between your lists. For example, your love of art and computer skills could help meet the world's need for user-friendly websites, leading to a career in web design. Alternatively, your passion for fitness and talent for teaching could help address the need for youth health education by making you a teen fitness coach.

Remember, finding your Ikigai isn't a race - it's more like a treasure hunt where the journey is just as valuable as the destination. Take time to explore different possibilities, try new things, and pay attention to what energizes you. Your perfect career sweet spot might be something you haven't even discovered yet, and that's what makes this journey so exciting!

Mapping Your Career DNA: Creating Your Personal Strength Profile

Now that we've explored the concept of Ikigai and natural talents, it's time to create your personal strength profile - think of it as mapping out your career DNA. Just like your biological DNA makes you unique, your career DNA is made up of specific strengths, skills, and qualities that make you stand out. Let's break this down into something practical you can use right now.

I love using the "**Strength Spotting Journal**" technique with my students. Here's how it works: For two weeks, keep track of moments when you feel particularly successful or energized. Maybe you crushed that group presentation, helped your friend understand a tricky math concept, or organized a fantastic fundraiser for your school club. These moments are like little signposts pointing toward your strengths.

One of my students, Jasmine, discovered something interesting through her Strength Spotting Journal. She noticed that whenever there was drama in her friends' group, everyone came to her for advice. At first, she didn't think this was anything special - it was just what she did. But as she tracked these moments, she realized she had a natural talent for understanding different perspectives and helping people find common ground. This insight led her to explore counseling and conflict resolution careers she'd never considered.

Key areas to track in your Strength Spotting Journal:

- Times when people ask for your help

- Projects or activities where you excel naturally

- Moments when you feel most confident

- Situations where you solve problems easily

- Activities that energize rather than drain you

Another powerful tool for mapping your career DNA is creating a "**Success Pattern Map**". Think about three accomplishments you're really proud of - they can be big or small. Now, break down exactly what you did to achieve each one. What skills did you use? What personal qualities helped you succeed? You'll often find patterns across successes pointing to your core strengths.

For example, when working with Alex, a quiet 15-year-old, we looked at three of his achievements: building a popular Discord server for his gaming community, helping his grandmother learn to use her new smartphone, and creating study guides that his classmates loved. The pattern? In each case, he showed a talent for making complex things simple and accessible to others - a valuable skill in many career paths, from technical writing to teaching to user experience design.

Here's a practical exercise to help you create your strength profile:

- Start with your top 3 achievements

- List the specific actions you took

- Identify the skills you used

- Note any patterns across different situations

- Consider how these skills might apply to different careers

Remember, your strength profile isn't just about what you're good at right now - it's also about potential. Maybe you're not the best public speaker yet, but you love sharing ideas with others and are willing to practice. That combination of interest and determination is part of your career DNA, too!

One thing I always emphasize with my students is that strengths come in many forms. You might be the person who's excellent at spotting details others miss, or maybe you're the one who can get people excited about new ideas. These qualities are just as important as traditional academic or technical skills.

Different types of strengths to consider:

- Technical skills (coding, design, writing)

- People skills (communication, leadership, empathy)

- Creative skills (problem-solving, innovation, artistic ability)

- Organizational skills (planning, time management, coordination)

- Analytical skills (research, critical thinking, pattern recognition)

As you map out your career DNA, don't forget to consider your growth zones - areas where you're not naturally talented but feel drawn to improve. Sometimes, these growth zones can point to careers you'd find fulfilling, even if they require more effort to develop the necessary skills.

The goal of creating your personal strength profile isn't to box yourself into specific career paths but to understand your unique combination of qualities. This understanding will become your compass as you explore different career options and help you recognize opportunities that align with your natural strengths.

Remember, your career DNA isn't set in stone - it evolves as you gain new experiences and develop new skills. The key is to start with a clear understanding of your current strengths while staying open to discovering new ones along the way. Think of it as creating a living document that grows and changes with you, helping guide your career choices at each step of your journey. As we wrap up this chapter on discovering your Career DNA, let's take a moment to reflect on what we've learned about understanding our unique strengths and passions. Remember Sarah's journey? She found a way to blend her artistic talents with her interest in healthcare, creating a career path that felt authentically *her*. Your journey might look different, but the principles remain the same - it's about discovering what makes you uniquely you.

Through our exploration of natural talents and the Ikigai framework, we've seen how understanding your Career DNA isn't about limiting yourself to one path but rather about recognizing the unique combination of skills, interests, and values that make you who you are. Whether you're someone like Tyler, who turned his TikTok skills into a thriving business, or like Jasmine, who discovered her talent for conflict resolution, your Career DNA is your personal roadmap to finding work that feels meaningful and fulfilling.

The Strength Spotting Journal and Success Pattern Map are tools you can start using right now to uncover your own career DNA. These aren't just exercises - they're the first steps in building a career that feels right for *you*. Remember, there's no rush to have it all figured out. Your Career DNA will continue to evolve as you gain new experiences and discover new interests.

As you move forward, remember that understanding your Career DNA is just the beginning. In the following chapters, we'll explore how to translate these insights into practical career choices, navigate the modern job landscape, and build the skills you need for success. But for now, focus on this fundamental truth: your unique combination of talents, passions, and values isn't a limitation - it's your superpower in finding work you'll love.

This week, take some time to start your own Strength Spotting Journal or create your Success Pattern Map. Pay attention to those moments when you feel most energized or when others consistently seek your help. These clues paint a picture of your Career DNA, and understanding this picture is your first step toward building a fulfilling career path.

Remember, just like biological DNA makes every person unique, your Career DNA is distinctly yours. There's no "right" or "wrong" combination - there's only what works for you. As you continue reading this book and exploring different career possibilities, let your Career DNA guide you in finding opportunities that align with your true identity.

In the next chapter, we'll dive into how the modern career landscape evolves and what that means for future opportunities. But for now, celebrate what you've learned about yourself and keep exploring those unique qualities that make up your Career DNA. Your journey to finding fulfilling work has already begun!

Chapter 2

Modern Career Landscape

Exploring Traditional, Digital, and Emerging Opportunities

Today's career landscape looks vastly different from what your parents or even older siblings might have experienced just a few years ago. While traditional careers like medicine, teaching, and engineering continue to evolve, entirely new professions are emerging at an unprecedented rate, creating exciting opportunities for those willing to embrace change and innovation. This transformation reshapes how we work and where and when we work, creating exciting possibilities for anyone willing to adapt and grow. Whether you're drawn to traditional careers evolving with technology or completely new digital professions, understanding these changes is crucial for making informed career choices.

One of the most significant shifts we're seeing is the rise of remote work and digital entrepreneurship. You no longer need to wait until graduation to start building your career - with a laptop and an internet connection, you can begin exploring opportunities right now. The possibilities are endless, from social media management to coding, content creation, and digital marketing.

During one of my career guidance workshops, I met Alex, a 17-year-old torn between following his family's traditional business path and his passion for social media content creation. His parents owned a local bookstore and expected him to take over, but Alex saw an opportunity to blend into both worlds. Over six months, he created a vibrant online presence for the family bookstore, launching a TikTok channel featuring book reviews, behind-the-scenes glimpses of bookstore life, and creative storytelling content. The store's online sales grew significantly, and Alex discovered he could honor his family's legacy while pioneering new digital marketing strategies. This experience taught him valuable lessons about how traditional businesses can thrive in the digital age, and he now helps other local businesses with their digital transformation while managing the modernized family bookstore. His story perfectly illustrates how modern careers often blend traditional and digital elements, creating unique opportunities for innovation and growth.

This workplace evolution doesn't mean traditional careers are disappearing – they're simply transforming. Teachers are becoming digital educators, healthcare professionals are embracing telemedicine, and retail businesses are developing omnichannel experiences. Even traditional trades like plumbing and electrical work now incorporate digital tools and online customer service platforms.

What's particularly exciting about this new landscape is how it levels the playing field for young people. You don't necessarily need years of experience or expensive degrees to start building a career. You need adaptability, digital literacy, and a willingness to embrace continuous learning. These skills, combined with your natural comfort with technology, give you a unique advantage in today's job market.

This chapter will explore evolving traditional careers and emerging opportunities that didn't exist just a few years ago. We'll look at how to prepare for jobs that might not even exist yet and, most importantly, how to develop the adaptable mindset needed to thrive in this dynamic environment. Whether you're interested in transforming a traditional career path or pioneering something entirely new, understanding the modern career landscape is your first step toward building a successful future.

Evolution of Traditional Careers in the Digital Age

Let's talk about how traditional careers are getting a major digital makeover! Remember when being a teacher meant standing in front of a classroom with a chalkboard? Now, educators are rocking virtual classrooms, creating digital content, and connecting with students worldwide through online platforms. It's like traditional careers are getting a cool tech upgrade, and trust me, this is something you'll want to understand for your future.

I recently worked with a student named Maya, who wanted to become a nurse like her mom. However, she discovered that modern nursing involves way more than patient care - it's about using health apps, managing electronic health records, and even providing care through telemedicine. Maya realized she needed to focus not just on medical knowledge but also on building strong tech skills to succeed in this evolved version of nursing.

Here are some key ways traditional careers are transforming:

- Healthcare professionals now use AI-assisted diagnostics and telemedicine platforms

- Teachers create digital curricula and manage online learning environments

- Accountants work with cloud-based software and automated reporting systems

- Lawyers use legal tech tools and digital case management systems

- Architects employ 3D modeling and virtual reality for designs

But here's the thing - this digital evolution isn't something to be scared of. Actually, it's creating some pretty exciting opportunities! Take journalism, for example. Traditional newspaper reporters are now digital storytellers who know how to create engaging content across multiple platforms. They're not just writing articles; they're producing podcasts, creating interactive web content, and engaging with readers through social media.

One of the coolest things about this evolution is how it's making traditional careers more flexible and accessible. You might think, *"But what if I'm not super tech-savvy?"* Don't worry! Most of these digital skills can be learned gradually, and many employers provide training for specific tools and platforms. The key is being open to learning and adapting as technology continues to evolve.

I remember working with Carlos, a high school junior interested in becoming an auto mechanic. He was surprised to learn that modern mechanics need to understand diagnostic software, work with electric vehicles, and even use augmented reality tools for repairs. Instead of being intimidated, Carlos got excited about combining his love for cars with new technology. He started taking online courses in automotive electronics while still in high school, giving him a head start in his career.

Here's something really important to understand: the digital transformation of traditional careers isn't about replacing human skills - it's about enhancing them. Your creativity, critical thinking, and people skills are still super valuable. Technology is just a tool that helps you work more efficiently and offers better services to people.

So what does this mean for you? As you're planning your career path, think about how you can embrace both traditional and digital skills in your chosen field. If you're interested in a traditional career, research how it's evolving and what new skills you might need. Look for opportunities to learn these skills through online courses, workshops, or even YouTube tutorials.

Remember, the most successful professionals in traditional careers are those who view digital transformation as an opportunity rather than a challenge. They stay curious, keep learning, and find innovative ways to use technology to do their jobs better. Whether you dream of becoming a teacher, doctor, lawyer, or any other traditional professional, understanding and embracing these digital changes will give you a serious advantage in your future career.

The best part? You're already ahead of the game! As a digital native, you have an intuitive understanding of technology that many seasoned professionals had to learn later in their careers. Use this advantage to reimagine traditional careers in exciting new ways. Who knows? You might even create new ways of working that nobody has thought of yet!

Emerging Digital Careers and Remote Work Opportunities

Ready to explore some seriously cool career opportunities that let you work from anywhere? Let's dive into the world of digital careers and remote work - it's way bigger and more exciting than you might think!

One of the most amazing things about our digital age is that you can start building your career right from your laptop. I recently mentored Zoe, a 16-year-old who turned her love of creating TikTok videos into a thriving social media management business. She started by helping local businesses with their social media presence while still in high school, and now she earns good money working flexible hours that fit her studies.

Here are some of the hottest digital careers that are perfect for tech-savvy teens:

- Content Creation and Management (Social media managers, YouTubers, bloggers)

- Digital Marketing (Email marketing, SEO specialists, PPC managers)

- Web Development and Design

- Virtual Assistance and Online Customer Service

- Digital Art and Graphic Design

But here's what's really cool - these aren't just side hustles. They're legitimate career paths that can grow into full-time professions. Take web development, for instance. You can start by building simple websites for local businesses or non-profits while learning, then progress to more complex projects as your skills grow.

The best part about digital careers? Many of them don't require a traditional college degree. What matters more is your portfolio of work and practical skills. Companies are increasingly focusing on what you can do rather than what degrees you have. This means you can start building your career while still figuring out your educational path.

Let's talk about remote work opportunities. Working remotely isn't just about sitting at home in your PJs (though that's definitely a perk!). It's about having the freedom to work from anywhere while connecting with people and companies worldwide. During my career guidance sessions, I've seen more and more teens interested in "laptop lifestyle" careers that offer this flexibility.

One of my favorite success stories is about Jamie, a student who started doing data entry work remotely during her junior year of high school. She used this experience to learn about different industries and build her professional network. By the time she graduated, she had developed her skills as a virtual assistant, specializing in helping small business owners manage their online presence.

Here's something crucial to understand about remote work: it requires different skills than traditional office jobs. You need to be self-motivated, organized, and good at communicating virtually. But these are exactly the kinds of skills that many of you are already developing through online school and social media!

Some key skills that will help you succeed in digital careers:

- Digital literacy and basic tech skills
- Time management and self-motivation
- Written and virtual communication
- Basic design and content creation abilities
- Problem-solving and adaptability

What's particularly exciting about digital careers is how they often overlap and complement each other. For example, if you start as a social media manager, you might naturally expand into content creation, graphic design, or digital marketing. This flexibility allows you to evolve your career as your interests and skills develop.

But let's be real - working remotely isn't always easy. It requires discipline and the ability to set boundaries between work and personal life. I always advise my students to start small, maybe with a part-time remote gig or freelance project, to see if this work style suits them.

The digital career landscape is constantly evolving, with new opportunities emerging all the time. Five years ago, nobody was hiring TikTok specialists or NFT artists! This means staying curious and continuing to learn is super important. Follow industry blogs, join online communities in your area of interest, and don't be afraid to experiment with new platforms and tools.

Remember, you don't have to wait until after graduation to start exploring these opportunities. Many digital careers can begin as after-school projects or weekend side hustles. This gives you the chance to try different things, build your skills, and maybe even earn some money while you figure out what you enjoy most.

The future of work is increasingly digital and remote, and you're in the perfect position to take advantage of these opportunities. Whether you're interested in creative work like content creation, technical work like coding, or business-focused roles like digital marketing, there's likely a digital career path that matches your interests and skills. The key is to start exploring, learning, and building your digital presence now!

Future-Proofing Your Career: Essential Skills for Tomorrow's Jobs

Let's talk about something super important - making sure your career can stand the test of time! Think of it like building a house that can weather any storm. You want to develop skills that'll keep you valuable in the job market, no matter what changes come your way.

I remember working with Ethan, a student who was laser-focused on learning one specific programming language because it was popular at the time. Through our career guidance sessions, we shifted his approach to focus on understanding programming concepts and problem-solving skills instead. Now, he can easily adapt to new programming languages as they emerge, making him much more valuable in the tech industry.

Here are some essential skills that'll help future-proof your career:

- Adaptability and Learning Agility (being able to pick up new skills quickly)

- Digital Literacy and Tech Fluency

- Critical Thinking and Problem-Solving

- Emotional Intelligence and Communication

- Creativity and Innovation

- Data Literacy and Analysis

But here's the thing - it's not just about collecting skills like Pokémon cards! It's about developing a mindset that embraces change and sees challenges as growth opportunities. The jobs of tomorrow might not even exist today, but if you have these foundational skills, you'll be ready to adapt and thrive.

I often use the 'skill stack' approach during my career workshops with students. Instead of trying to master everything, focus on building a unique combination of complementary skills. For example, if you're interested in design, don't just learn graphic design software - add skills in user psychology, basic coding, and project management. This combination makes you much more valuable and adaptable in the job market.

One of the most powerful ways to future-proof your career is to become what I call a 'T-shaped professional.' Imagine the letter T - you want to have broad knowledge across many areas (the horizontal line) while also developing deep expertise in one or two areas (the vertical line). This gives you both flexibility and specialization.

I worked with Sofia, who loved art but worried about job security. Instead of just focusing on traditional art skills, she developed a skill stack that included digital art, UI/UX design, and basic web development. Now, she's able to adapt to different roles in the creative industry, from digital illustration to web design, making her much more resilient to market changes.

Here's something crucial to understand: the most future-proof careers aren't necessarily the most technical ones. While tech skills are important, human skills like empathy, creativity, and complex problem-solving are becoming increasingly valuable. These are skills that AI and automation can't easily replicate.

Want to start future-proofing your career now? Here are some practical steps:

- Stay curious and keep learning (try free online courses, YouTube tutorials, podcasts)

- Practice adapting to change (try learning new tools or taking on different types of projects)

- Build your digital literacy (experiment with new apps and platforms)

- Develop your emotional intelligence (practice active listening and understanding others)

- Get comfortable with data (learn basic analytics and how to interpret information)

Remember, future-proofing isn't about predicting the future - it's about being ready for whatever comes your way. Think of it like having a Swiss Army knife of skills rather than just one specialized tool. The more versatile you are, the better equipped you'll be to handle changes in the job market.

One of the best ways to stay future-ready is to keep an eye on emerging trends while building strong foundational skills. Join online communities in your areas of interest, follow industry blogs, and connect with professionals who inspire you. But don't get overwhelmed trying to chase every new trend - focus on understanding the underlying principles and skills that make people successful across different fields.

The most exciting part? You're already ahead of the game in many ways. Growing up in a digital world, you naturally understand many concepts that older professionals have to learn later in life. Use this advantage! Your intuitive understanding of digital tools and ability to adapt quickly to new technology are incredibly valuable skills in today's job market.

Remember, future-proofing your career isn't a one-time thing - it's an ongoing learning, adapting, and growing process. Stay curious, remain flexible, and never stop developing new skills. The future might be uncertain, but with the proper preparation, you can be ready for whatever opportunities come your way! As we wrap up our exploration of the modern career landscape, I hope you're excited about the incredible opportunities that lie ahead. Whether you're drawn to traditional careers evolving with technology or completely new digital professions, remember that your career journey is uniquely yours to shape.

Let's take a moment to reflect on the key insights we've covered. We've seen how traditional careers transform through technology, creating exciting new healthcare, education, and business possibilities. We've explored emerging digital careers that didn't even exist a few years ago and discussed essential skills that will help you stay valuable in tomorrow's job market.

Remember Alex's story from the beginning of this chapter? His success in blending traditional business with digital innovation shows us that we don't always have to choose between old and new – sometimes, the most exciting opportunities come from combining both. Like Alex, you have the chance to pioneer new approaches in whatever field interests you.

As you move forward, remember that adaptability is the most important skill you can develop. The job market will continue to evolve, and new opportunities will emerge that we can't even imagine yet. That's not something to fear—it's something to get excited about! Your generation has a natural advantage in understanding and adapting to digital changes.

Before we move on to the next chapter, here's a challenge for you: Take some time to research how your dream career might evolve in the next five to ten years. What new skills might you need? What technologies could change how that job is done? Understanding these potential changes can help you prepare for success.

Remember, whether you're interested in transforming a traditional career or pioneering something entirely new, your unique perspective and skills are valuable. The modern career landscape might be changing rapidly, but that change brings unprecedented opportunities for those willing to embrace it.

In the next chapter, we'll explore different educational paths and how to choose the right one for your career goals. But for now, take some time to think about how you might want to combine traditional and digital elements in your own career journey. The future of work is yours to shape, and it's looking brighter and more exciting than ever before.

Chapter 3

THE SMART PATH FORWARD

College, Trade School, or Alternative Routes?

The path to your dream career isn't always a straight line, and contrary to popular belief, there isn't a one-size-fits-all approach to post-high school education. Whether considering a four-year university, trade school, apprenticeship, or alternative route, understanding how each option aligns with your career goals and personal circumstances is key. Remember that feeling of being pulled in different directions when choosing your path forward? You're not alone. Like many teens today, you might wonder if college is the only route to a successful career or if other options could better fit your goals and circumstances.

Let me share a story that perfectly illustrates this journey of discovery. In my career guidance practice, I worked with twin brothers, Marcus and Michael. Although they had utterly different career aspirations, they faced similar pressure to attend traditional four-year colleges. Marcus was passionate about automotive technology and dreamed of owning his own shop, while Michael loved computer programming and wanted to work in tech. Their parents insisted they both attend university, viewing it as the only path to success.

Through our sessions, we explored different educational options that aligned with their individual goals. Marcus discovered a prestigious automotive trade school program offering technical training and business management courses. Meanwhile, Michael found a coding boot camp combined with online computer science courses that would fast-track his entry into tech while allowing him to build a portfolio of real projects. Today, Marcus runs a successful auto repair business after completing his trade school program, while Michael works as a software developer after completing his alternative education path. Their story illustrates how different educational routes can lead to successful careers when aligned with personal goals and interests.

Their journey highlights something crucial: there is no one-size-fits-all approach to building your future. The landscape of education and career preparation has transformed dramatically in recent years. Trade schools, apprenticeships, coding boot camps, and entrepreneurship programs now stand alongside traditional college degrees as viable pathways to successful careers.

In this chapter, we'll explore these various paths in detail, helping you understand the pros and cons of each option. We'll look at factors like cost, time investment, and potential return on investment - because, let's face it, these practical considerations matter. You'll learn to evaluate different educational options based on your specific career goals, financial situation, and personal circumstances.

We'll break down common myths about different educational paths and provide you with tools to make informed decisions about your future. Whether you lean toward a traditional four-year degree, considering a trade school, or thinking about jumping straight into entrepreneurship, this chapter will help you understand what each path really entails and how to make the most of whichever route you choose.

Most importantly, we'll discuss aligning your educational choices with your career aspirations while considering factors like learning style, financial resources, and time commitment. At the end of the day, the best path forward is the one that works for *you*—not what worked for your parents, your siblings, or your friends.

So, let's dive in and explore the various routes you can take toward your dream career. Remember, it's not about finding the "perfect" path - it's about finding the path that best aligns with your goals, values, and circumstances.

Understanding the ROI: Comparing Costs and Benefits of Different Educational Paths

Let's talk about something that might sound boring but is super important - ROI or Return on Investment. Think of it like this: if you invest your time and money into education after high school, you want to ensure you're getting the best value possible, right?

When I work with teens like you, I often use the example of buying a car. Wouldn't you spend $50,000 on a car worth $20,000? The same principle applies to your education. Every educational path - whether it's college, trade school, or specialized training - is an investment in your future, and it's crucial to understand what you're getting for your money and time.

Let's break down some real numbers and options:

<u>Traditional 4-Year College</u>

- Average cost: $20,000-$40,000 per year
- Time investment: 4+ years
- Potential benefits: Higher lifetime earnings, broader career options
- Additional considerations: Student loan debt, delayed earning years

<u>Trade School/Vocational Training</u>

- Average cost: $5,000-$15,000 per year
- Time investment: 6 months to 2 years
- Potential benefits: Faster entry into the workforce, specific skill certification
- Additional considerations: Lower initial costs, earlier earning potential

<u>Coding Bootcamps/Specialized Training</u>

- Average cost: $10,000-$20,000 total
- Time investment: 3-6 months
- Potential benefits: Quick skill acquisition, immediate job market entry
- Additional considerations: Industry-specific focus, rapid career transition

But here's the thing - ROI isn't just about money. During my career guidance sessions, I worked with a student named Tyler, who was torn between attending an expensive private university and starting at a community college.

We looked beyond just the dollar signs and considered factors like:

- Quality of specific programs
- Networking opportunities
- Internship connections
- Location and living costs
- Available scholarships and financial aid
- Career support services

Tyler decided to start at a community college, saving nearly $30,000 in his first two years while maintaining the option to transfer to a four-year university later. He used the money he saved to participate in coding boot camps during summer breaks, building a unique skill set that made him stand out to employers.

Here's a practical way to evaluate your own educational ROI:

- Research starting salaries in your chosen field
- Calculate total education costs (including living expenses)
- Consider the time until you start earning
- Factor in potential student loan payments
- Look at job market demand and growth

Remember, the highest-cost option isn't always the best, and the lowest-cost option isn't always the worst. The key is finding the sweet spot where your investment aligns with your career goals and financial reality.

One often overlooked aspect of ROI is the "hidden" benefits of different educational paths. For instance, trade schools usually offer programs that include hands-on experience and industry certifications, while traditional colleges might offer extensive alumni networks and research opportunities. These factors can significantly impact long-term career success.

Consider creating a personal ROI spreadsheet to compare different paths. Include both quantitative factors (costs, potential earnings) and qualitative factors (work-life balance, job satisfaction, career growth potential).

This will help you make a more informed decision about your educational investment.

The most important thing to remember is that ROI varies from person to person. What's an excellent investment for your best friend might not be your best choice. Your ROI calculation should reflect your personal goals, financial situation, and career aspirations. Take time to really think about what success means to you. It's not just about the biggest paycheck but about finding a path that leads to financial stability and personal fulfillment.

Trade Schools and Apprenticeships: Skills-Based Career Development

Let's talk about one of the most exciting (and often overlooked) paths to a fantastic career - trade schools and apprenticeships! If you love hands-on learning and want to jump into a well-paying career without spending four years in a classroom, this section is definitely for you.

I remember working with Chris, a student who felt totally lost because everyone kept pushing him toward college, even though he loved working with his hands and solving practical problems. During our career guidance sessions, we explored trade school options, and his eyes lit up when he discovered that skilled electricians often earn more than many college graduates - without the student loan debt! Today, Chris is halfway through his electrical apprenticeship, earning while he learns, and already has job offers lined up.

Let's break down some of the most popular trade schools and apprenticeship paths:

- Skilled Trades
- Electrician
- Plumber
- HVAC Technician
- Carpenter
- Welder
- Healthcare Trades

- Dental Hygienist

- Medical Laboratory Technician

- Respiratory Therapist

- Licensed Practical Nurse

- Technology Trades

- IT Support Specialist

- Network Technician

- Automotive Technology

- Aviation Maintenance

One of the most significant advantages of choosing a trade school or apprenticeship path is the "earn while you learn" approach. Unlike traditional colleges, where you're paid to learn, many apprenticeships pay you a salary while you train. Plus, you're getting real-world experience from day one, which is something employers absolutely love.

Here's something that might surprise you - many trade school graduates start their careers earning $40,000 to $60,000 annually, and experienced tradespeople often earn six-figure incomes. The best part? Most trade programs can be completed in 6-24 months, meaning you could start your career while your friends are halfway through their college degrees.

But let's be honest - trade school isn't just about making money quickly. It's about finding a career path that matches your learning style and interests. If you're someone who learns better by doing rather than sitting in lectures, trade school might be perfect for you. Plus, many trades offer incredible opportunities for entrepreneurship - just think about how many successful plumbing or electrical businesses are out there!

Here's what you should consider when exploring trade schools and apprenticeships:

- Program Length and Schedule

- Cost and Financial Aid Options

- Certification Requirements

- Job Placement Rates

- Apprenticeship Opportunities

One of my favorite success stories is about Maria, a student who discovered her passion for welding during a high school workshop. Everyone expected her to follow the 'traditional' college path, but she chose to enroll in a welding program instead. Within 18 months, she had completed her certification and landed a job at a major manufacturing company. Two years later, she started her own mobile welding business and now earns more than most of her college-educated friends.

The skilled trades are experiencing a severe shortage of workers right now, which means there are tons of opportunities for young people who want to enter these fields. Many companies are even offering signing bonuses and additional training benefits to attract new talents.

If you're interested in exploring trade schools or apprenticeships, start by:

- Researching programs in your area

- Talking to people already working in the trade

- Checking out local unions and trade organizations

- Looking into apprenticeship programs

- Visiting trade schools and watching demonstrations

Remember, choosing a trade school or apprenticeship doesn't mean you can't go to college later if you want to. Many people start in the trades and then use their earnings to fund additional education or start their own businesses. The key is finding a path that works for you and your goals.

Don't let anyone tell you that trade school is a 'lesser' option than college - that's totally outdated thinking! In today's world, skilled trades are some of the most stable, well-paying careers you can choose. Plus, these are jobs that can't be outsourced or replaced by AI - people will always need electricians, plumbers, welders, and other skilled tradespeople.

The future of trade careers looks super bright, with new technologies creating exciting opportunities in traditional fields. For example, modern auto mechanics need to understand complex computer systems and HVAC technicians must work with smart home technology. These aren't just conventional manual labor jobs anymore - they're high-tech careers that combine hands-on skills with cutting-edge technology.

Alternative Routes: Entrepreneurship, Certifications, and Self-Directed Learning

Ready to explore some exciting alternatives to the traditional education path? Let's dive into the world of entrepreneurship, professional certifications, and self-directed learning - because sometimes the most interesting journeys don't follow the usual map!

One of my favorite stories comes from working with Jade, a 16-year-old who was passionate about sustainable fashion. Instead of waiting for college to start her career, she launched an online vintage clothing business from her bedroom while completing free online business courses. Within a year, she had built a thriving Instagram shop while earning professional certifications in digital marketing and e-commerce - all before graduating high school!

Let's explore some alternative routes that might be perfect for you:

- Online learning platforms
- Coursera, edX, and LinkedIn Learning
- Industry-specific training programs
- YouTube tutorials and educational channels
- Coding boot camps
- Professional certifications
- Digital marketing certifications
- IT and tech certifications
- Project management credentials
- Design and creative certifications

- Entrepreneurship opportunities
- Online businesses
- Service-based enterprises
- Content creation
- Social media management

Here's something cool - many of these alternatives can be started while you're still in high school, giving you a head start on your career. Plus, they often cost way less than traditional college and can be completed at your own pace.

Let's talk about self-directed learning for a minute. Think of it like being the CEO of your own education - you decide what to learn, when to learn it, and how to apply it. This approach is perfect for go-getters who love taking control of their own progress.

During my career guidance sessions, I worked with Marcus, who combined his love for gaming with entrepreneurship. He started learning game development through online courses while earning certifications in digital marketing. Today, he runs a successful gaming YouTube channel and creates tutorials for other young developers, all without setting foot in a traditional classroom.

Here are some practical steps to start your alternative education journey:

- Research and choose relevant certifications in your field of interest
- Create a learning schedule that works with your current commitments
- Join online communities related to your chosen path
- Start building a portfolio of projects or work samples
- Network with others who've taken similar routes

One of the biggest advantages of these alternative routes is flexibility. You can test different paths without committing huge amounts of time or money. Plus, you're building real-world skills and experience that employers value - sometimes even more than traditional degrees.

But here's the real talk - alternative routes require serious self-discipline and motivation. You won't have professors setting deadlines or classmates to study with. Instead, you'll need to be your own motivation coach and time manager. But don't worry - that's actually excellent preparation for any career!

Consider starting with a 'mini-portfolio' approach:

- Choose one certification to pursue
- Start a small side project or business
- Document your learning journey
- Connect with mentors in your field
- Build an online presence

Remember, these alternative routes aren't "lesser" choices - just different paths to success. Many successful entrepreneurs and professionals have taken non-traditional routes to achieve their goals. The key is finding the path that matches your learning style, goals, and circumstances.

Here's a pro tip: combine different alternative routes for maximum impact. For example, you might earn a digital marketing certification while starting a small social media management business, then use those skills to build your own brand or help other businesses grow.

The beauty of alternative routes is that they often allow you to start earning while learning. Unlike traditional education, where you typically wait 4+ years to start your career, many of these paths let you begin building your professional life right away.

And don't forget about the power of community learning. Join online forums, Discord servers, or local meetup groups related to your interests. These communities can provide support, advice, and even job opportunities as you progress on your alternative path.

The future of education and career development is becoming increasingly flexible and personalized. By exploring alternative routes now, you're not just preparing for today's job market - you're positioning yourself for whatever opportunities tomorrow might bring. Whether you dream of being an entrepreneur, a digital nomad, or a specialized professional, there's an alternative path that can help you get there. As we wrap up our exploration of educational pathways, remember that the journey to your dream career isn't about following someone else's roadmap - it's about creating your own path that aligns with your goals, values, and circumstances. Whether you're drawn to trade school, traditional college, entrepreneurship, or a combination of paths, what matters most is making an informed decision that works for YOU.

Think back to Marcus and Michael's story - two brothers who found success through entirely different routes. Their experience shows us there's no single "right way" to build a successful career. While Marcus thrived in trade school and built a successful automotive business, Michael found his perfect fit in a combination of coding boot camps and online courses. Both brothers are successful today because they chose paths that matched their individual strengths and interests.

Let's be honest - making decisions about your future can feel overwhelming. You might be wrestling with questions about college costs, worried about making the "wrong" choice or feeling pressure from family and friends to follow a specific path. These concerns are totally normal! What's important is understanding that your educational journey should be as unique as you are.

Remember those key points we covered? Whether it's calculating the ROI of different educational options, exploring trade schools and apprenticeships, or considering alternative routes like entrepreneurship and self-directed learning - you now have the tools to evaluate which path might work best for you. The modern job market offers more flexibility and opportunities than ever before, and there's no shame in taking an unconventional route to success.

As you move forward, keep in mind that your initial choice isn't a life sentence. Many successful professionals change directions multiple times throughout their careers. What matters is starting somewhere and remaining open to learning and growth. Maybe you'll start with a certification program and later decide to pursue a degree, or perhaps you'll combine trade school training with entrepreneurship - the possibilities are endless!

Before we move on, take a moment to reflect on your own Career DNA and how it aligns with the different educational paths we've discussed. Remember that success isn't just about the credentials you earn - it's about finding a path that allows you to grow, learn, and ultimately build a career that brings you both personal satisfaction and financial stability.

You've got this! Whether you choose college, trade school, or forge your own path through alternative routes, what matters most is making an informed decision based on your unique situation and goals. The world of work is changing rapidly, and having the courage to choose your own path - even if it's different from what others expect - might just be your greatest strength.

In the next chapter, we'll explore how to leverage modern technology and AI to create your own business opportunities, building on the educational foundation you choose to pursue. Get ready to discover how the digital revolution creates exciting new possibilities for young entrepreneurs!

Chapter 4

Digital Success

Leveraging AI and Technology for Your Own Business

In today's digital age, starting your own business doesn't require a large investment or years of experience - just a smartphone, an internet connection, and the right knowledge of leveraging technology. The rise of artificial intelligence and digital tools has created unprecedented opportunities for young entrepreneurs to turn their ideas into profitable ventures while still in their teens. The rapid advancement of AI tools and digital platforms has created a landscape where young entrepreneurs can start businesses with minimal upfront investment, focusing instead on creativity and innovative technology use. Whether you're interested in e-commerce, digital marketing, content creation, affiliate marketing, or providing online services, the digital world offers countless opportunities for teens to build successful ventures.

But it's not just about using technology – it's about understanding how to blend AI capabilities with your unique human touch to create something valuable. Think of AI as your digital assistant, helping you work smarter and more efficiently while you focus on building relationships and solving real problems for your customers.

During one of my teen entrepreneurship workshops, I met Jamie, a 16-year-old passionate about helping local small businesses but unsure how to turn this into a viable business idea. Using AI tools and digital platforms, Jamie created a service helping small local restaurants improve their online presence. She used AI writing tools to craft engaging social media content, implemented basic chatbots for customer service, and utilized design AI to create eye-catching graphics. Within six months, Jamie built a successful digital marketing agency serving five local restaurants, managing their social media presence while still maintaining her school responsibilities. Her story demonstrates how combining technological tools with personal passion can create viable business opportunities, even for young entrepreneurs. The key to her success wasn't just using technology but understanding how to blend AI capabilities with human creativity and personal connection to deliver value to her clients.

This chapter explores how you can leverage AI and digital tools to start your own business venture. We'll look at practical ways to identify opportunities in the digital space, understand the basics of AI tools and applications, and develop the essential skills needed for digital entrepreneurship. Most importantly, we'll focus on maintaining a crucial balance between automation and human touch. While AI can enhance your business operations, your unique perspective and creativity will truly set you apart.

Remember, starting a digital business isn't just about making money; it's about creating value while learning real-world skills that will benefit you throughout your career. Whether you're interested in becoming a full-time entrepreneur or want to develop a side hustle while pursuing other career paths, understanding how to harness digital tools and AI can open doors you might never have imagined.

Understanding AI Tools: From Chatbots to Content Creation

Let's dive into the world of AI tools - they're not just fancy tech buzzwords but actual digital assistants that can help you build and grow your business. Think of AI tools as your personal team of helpers that can tackle everything from writing and design to customer service and data analysis.

One of the most practical AI tools you'll encounter is the chatbot. These digital assistants can handle customer questions 24/7, giving you the freedom to focus on other aspects of your business. For example, suppose you're running an online store. In that case, a chatbot can help customers track their orders, answer common questions about your products, and even guide them through the buying process - all while you're sleeping or studying for tomorrow's test!

Content creation AI tools are another game-changer for young entrepreneurs. These tools can help you brainstorm ideas, write social media posts, and even create basic graphics. But here's the important part - they're not meant to replace your creativity but to enhance it. Think of them as a starting point you can build upon with your unique voice and style.

Here are some key AI tools that can help you get started:

- Writing Assistants: Help with everything from blog posts to product descriptions

- Image Generation Tools: Create custom graphics and illustrations

- Social Media Managers: Schedule and optimize your posts
- Video Creation Tools: Edit and enhance your video content
- Research Tools: Gather and analyze market data

But remember, while these tools are powerful, they're not magic wands. The key is understanding their limitations and knowing when to rely on your human touch. For instance, while an AI writing tool can help you draft a social media post, you'll need to review and personalize it to match your brand's voice and connect with your audience authentically.

One of my students, Marcus, started a homework-help service using AI tools to streamline his operations. He used a chatbot to handle initial student inquiries and schedule sessions, as well as AI writing tools to create study guides. However, he quickly learned that the real value came from combining these AI capabilities with his own teaching skills and personal connection with students. His business thrived because he found the right balance between automation and a personal touch.

When using AI tools, keep these essential guidelines in mind:

- Always review and edit AI-generated content
- Maintain your unique voice and perspective
- Use AI for repetitive tasks to free up your creative time
- Stay updated on tool capabilities and limitations
- Prioritize data privacy and security

The exciting part about AI tools is that they're becoming more accessible and user-friendly daily. You don't need to be a tech genius to use them - just curious and willing to learn. Start small by experimenting with one or two tools that align with your business needs. Maybe begin with a simple writing assistant for your social media posts or a basic chatbot for customer service.

As you grow more comfortable with these tools, you can explore more advanced features and combinations. The key is to view AI tools as enablers rather than replacements - they're here to amplify your capabilities, not take over your business. Your unique insights, creativity, and human connection will always be your greatest business assets.

Remember, the goal isn't to automate everything but to use AI tools strategically to build a more efficient and scalable business while maintaining the personal touch that makes your venture unique. Whether starting a social media management service, an online tutoring platform, or a digital art business, understanding and effectively using AI tools can give you a significant advantage in today's digital marketplace.

Digital Business Models: Identifying Your Online Niche

Finding your perfect online niche isn't about jumping on the latest TikTok trend or copying what's already out there. It's about discovering where your unique skills and interests intersect with what people actually need and want. Think of it as finding your spot in a digital marketplace where you can truly shine and make a difference.

When I work with teens exploring digital business ideas, I always start by asking them to consider **three key questions:**

- What problems can you solve or needs can you fill?
- What unique skills or perspectives do you bring?
- What topics or activities get you excited enough to stick with them long-term?

Let's break down some popular digital business models that teens can explore:

- Content Creation: Blogging, vlogging, podcasting
- Digital Products: Online courses, ebooks, templates
- Services: Virtual assistance, social media management, tutoring
- E-commerce: Dropshipping, print-on-demand, digital downloads
- Community Building: Membership sites, online communities

One of my favorite success stories comes from a student named Riley. She combined her love of bullet journaling with her organizational skills. Instead of selling physical journals (which would have required inventory and shipping), she created digital planning templates and taught online workshops about productivity for fellow students. She found her niche by focusing on helping other teens manage their time and reduce stress through creative planning.

The key to finding your niche is understanding that you don't need to appeal to everyone—you just need to serve your specific audience well. Think about what makes you different. Maybe you're great at explaining complex topics in simple terms, or perhaps you have a unique perspective on fashion that resonates with other teens.

Here are some practical steps to help you identify your digital business niche:

- Research Potential Markets: Look for gaps in existing services

- Test Your Ideas: Start small and gather feedback

- Analyze Competition: Study what others are doing and how you can be different

- Consider Your Resources: Choose a niche you can serve with your current skills and tools

Remember, your age can actually be an advantage in the digital space. You understand your generation's needs and preferences in a way that older entrepreneurs might not. Use this insight to create solutions that truly resonate with your peers.

When exploring different business models, consider starting with one with low overhead costs that can be managed around your school schedule. For instance, if you're interested in graphic design, you might start by creating and selling digital templates or offering design services to local businesses. This allows you to gradually build your skills and client base without overwhelming yourself.

Don't be afraid to combine different elements from various business models. The digital world is flexible enough to allow for creative combinations. For example, you might start a YouTube channel about study tips (content creation) while selling digital study planners (products) and offering one-on-one tutoring sessions (services).

The most successful digital businesses often start small and grow organically. Begin by focusing on one specific problem or need, and let your business evolve based on feedback from your audience. Pay attention to what your customers are asking for and be willing to adapt your offerings accordingly.

As you explore different niches, keep in mind that the digital landscape is constantly changing. What works today might need to be adjusted tomorrow. That's why it's important to choose a niche you're genuinely interested in. Your passion will help you stay motivated to keep learning and adapting as the market evolves.

Finally, don't forget about the importance of authenticity in your chosen niche. In today's digital world, people can quickly spot when someone isn't genuine. Share your real experiences, be honest about what you know (and don't know), and let your personality shine through in your business. This authenticity will help you build trust with your audience and create a sustainable business that grows with you.

Building Your Digital Presence: Social Media Strategy and Online Marketing

In today's digital world, your online presence is like your virtual business card - it's often the first impression potential customers or clients will have of you. But don't worry if you're not sure where to start! Building a strong digital presence is a skill you can learn, just like any other.

Let me share a story about one of my students, Zoe, who started her digital journey feeling overwhelmed by all the different social media platforms and marketing options. She wanted to promote her handmade jewelry business but didn't know where to focus her efforts. Together, we developed a simple but effective strategy: instead of trying to be everywhere at once, she chose two platforms where her target audience - other creative teens - spent most of their time.

Here are some key elements to consider when building your digital presence:

- Platform Selection: Choose social media platforms that align with your business and audience

- Content Strategy: Plan what you'll share and when you'll share it

- Brand Voice: Develop a consistent way of communicating that reflects your personality

- Visual Identity: Create a cohesive look across all your platforms

- Engagement Plan: Decide how you'll interact with your audience

Remember, you don't need to be on every social media platform. It's better to do a great job on one or two than a mediocre job on five or six. Think about where your target audience spends their time and focus your efforts there.

When it comes to content creation, think about the 80/20 rule: 80% of your content should provide value to your audience (such as tips, insights, or entertainment), while 20% can be promotional. This helps build trust and keeps your followers engaged. For example, if you run a tutoring service, you might share study tips, time management hacks, motivational content, and posts about your services.

One of the biggest mistakes I see teens make is trying to copy exactly what successful accounts are doing. While it's great to draw inspiration from others, your unique voice and perspective will make you stand out. Share your journey, including the challenges and victories - people connect with authenticity more than perfection.

Here are some practical steps to start building your digital presence:

- Create a content calendar to plan your posts
- Use free design tools to create professional-looking graphics
- Engage with your audience by responding to comments and messages
- Track what content performs best and adjust accordingly
- Stay consistent with your posting schedule

Zoe found that sharing behind-the-scenes content of her jewelry-making process got much more engagement than just posting product photos. Her followers loved seeing the creative process and learning about different techniques. This not only helped her build a loyal following but also established her expertise in her craft.

When it comes to online marketing, start with these foundational strategies:

- Hashtag Research: Find and use relevant hashtags to increase your visibility
- Collaboration Opportunities: Partner with complementary businesses or creators

- Story Features: Use platform features like Instagram Stories or TikTok to show your personality

- Customer Testimonials: Share positive feedback and success stories

- Community Building: Create opportunities for your followers to interact with each other

Don't get discouraged if growth seems slow initially - building a genuine following takes time. Focus on creating value for your audience and being consistent with your efforts. It's better to have 100 engaged followers who love what you do than 1,000 who never interact with your content.

As your digital presence grows, remember to stay true to your values and maintain professional boundaries. While it's important to be personal and relatable, you don't need to share everything online. Think about the image you want to project and how it aligns with your long-term goals.

Finally, don't forget to review and adjust your strategy regularly. The digital world moves fast, and what works today might need tweaking tomorrow. Stay curious, keep learning, and be willing to experiment with new approaches while staying true to your core message and values. As we wrap up our exploration of digital entrepreneurship and AI-powered business opportunities, remember that starting your own digital venture isn't just about using the latest tech tools - it's about finding creative ways to solve problems and add value to people's lives.

Through this chapter, we've discovered how AI can be your digital assistant, helping you work smarter and more efficiently while you focus on building meaningful connections with your customers. From Jamie's success story with her digital marketing agency to practical strategies for leveraging AI tools, we've seen how combining technology with human creativity can create fantastic opportunities for young entrepreneurs.

Key Takeaways

The key takeaways from this chapter will help you navigate your own digital business journey:

- Start small and focus on solving real problems for real people

- Use AI tools to enhance your capabilities, not replace your unique perspective

- Build an authentic digital presence that reflects your values and personality

- Focus on creating value while maintaining the human touch in your business

- Stay adaptable and willing to learn as technology continues to evolve

Remember, your age isn't a limitation - it's actually an advantage in the digital space. You understand your generation's needs and preferences in ways that older entrepreneurs might not, giving you unique insights into creating solutions that truly resonate with your peers.

As you move forward with your own digital business ideas, don't feel pressured to figure everything out at once. Start with one platform, one tool, or one service that excites you. Learn from your experiences, adjust your approach based on feedback, and, most importantly, stay true to your authentic self as you build your digital presence.

The digital business landscape will continue to evolve, but the fundamental principles we've discussed - solving real problems, maintaining authenticity, and balancing technology with human connection - will always be relevant. Whether you dream of starting a social media agency, creating digital products, or offering online services, you now have the foundation to begin your entrepreneurial journey.

Your future in digital business starts here - not with perfect plans or fancy technology, but with your unique ideas and willingness to learn and grow. Take that first step, experiment with the tools and strategies we've discussed, and remember that every successful digital entrepreneur started exactly where you are now - with an idea and the courage to try something new.

Leave A Review

Thank You!

If this book resonated with you or supported you in any way, you're warmly invited to leave a **review** on the platform where you purchased this book — reviews help other readers discover books like this.

If you'd like, you can also access an **optional companion resource** created to support and complement your reading experience.

Scan Me: REVIEW and download optional COMPANION RESOURCE

Chapter 5

Building Your Experience Bank

Real-World Skills and International Experience That Matter

Your future career success isn't just about what you know from books - it's about the real-world experiences you collect along the way. Think of these experiences as deposits in your personal skills bank, each one adding value to your professional worth and making you more attractive to future employers or clients. Just like a savings account grows with each deposit, your experience bank becomes richer with every opportunity you seize - whether volunteering at a local shelter, completing an online certification, or participating in a virtual international exchange program. In today's competitive world, employers and colleges look beyond grades to see what real-world experiences you've accumulated.

Think about it - when was the last time someone asked you about your test scores versus what actual skills and experiences you bring to the table? The truth is, while academic achievements matter, it's your practical experiences that often make the difference in standing out from the crowd. These experiences don't just pad your resume; they help you discover what you truly enjoy (and what you don't), build confidence, and develop crucial soft skills that no textbook can teach.

During a career guidance session, I worked with Emma, a shy 15-year-old who worried about her lack of work experience. Together, we developed a strategic plan to build her experience bank. She started by volunteering at her local library's children's reading program, which helped develop her communication and leadership skills. She joined a virtual cultural exchange program, where she connected with peers from different countries to gain international exposure without traveling. Emma documented each experience, skill learned, and artistic insight gained in a digital portfolio. Within a year, she had transformed from a hesitant teenager into a confident young leader with impressive experience in public speaking, cross-cultural communication, and digital collaboration. When applying for a competitive summer internship at age 16, Emma's unique combination of local volunteer work and virtual international experience made her application stand out. Her story demonstrates how strategic experience-building, even at a young age, can create valuable opportunities and build confidence for future career success.

The beauty of building your experience bank is that you don't need to wait until you're older or have a formal job. Every experience, no matter how small it might seem, can contribute to your professional growth. Whether it's managing your school's social media account, organizing a fundraiser, or learning a new programming language online, these experiences are valuable deposits in your professional journey.

In this chapter, we'll explore various ways to gain meaningful experience while still in school, from traditional volunteering and internships to innovative virtual opportunities and international experiences. You'll learn to identify opportunities that align with your interests, make the most of each experience, and effectively showcase your growing skills to future employers or college admissions officers. Remember, the goal isn't just to collect experiences like badges but to build a thoughtful collection of skills and insights that will serve as stepping stones toward your career goals.

Strategic Volunteering and Internships: Building Professional Experience While in School

Let's talk about one of the most powerful ways to build your experience bank is strategic volunteering and internships. I know what you might think: *"Isn't volunteering just something to make my college application look good?"* Trust me, it's so much more than that! When done strategically, volunteering and internships can be your secret weapon for gaining real-world experience, building professional connections, and discovering what you truly enjoy doing.

Think of strategic volunteering as test-driving different careers without the pressure of a full-time job. It's your chance to explore various fields, develop practical skills, and maybe even discover passion areas you never knew existed. The key word here is "strategic" - we're not just talking about random acts of kindness (though those are great too!), but carefully chosen opportunities that align with your career interests.

Here are some clever ways to approach volunteering and internships:

- Look for opportunities that match your career interests (like helping at an animal shelter if you're interested in veterinary medicine)
- Focus on roles where you can learn specific skills (such as social

media management for a nonprofit)

- Seek positions with increasing responsibility over time
- Choose organizations that offer mentorship or training programs
- Consider virtual volunteering opportunities to gain experience in digital collaboration

The beauty of strategic volunteering is that you can start small and gradually take on more responsibility. For example, you might begin by helping with basic tasks at a local nonprofit's social media account, then progress to creating content and eventually managing their entire online presence. Each step builds your skills and confidence while providing a real experience you can add to your resume.

One of my students, Carlos, turned his passion for video editing into valuable experience by volunteering to create promotional videos for local nonprofits. He started with simple event recordings but soon advanced to producing professional-quality content. Not only did he build an impressive portfolio, but he also made connections that led to paid freelance work. The best part? He was able to do all this while still in high school, fitting it around his studies and other activities.

When it comes to internships, many teens think they're only available during college years. Not true! More companies offer high school internship programs, including virtual options that make them more accessible than ever. These opportunities can provide invaluable insights into potential career paths and help you develop professional skills early on.

Here are some practical tips for finding and landing internships while still in school:

- Start with local businesses and organizations in your area of interest
- Check if your school has partnerships with any companies offering internships
- Look for summer programs specifically designed for high school students
- Consider reaching out to family, friends or relatives who work in fields you're interested in

- Don't overlook virtual internship opportunities that offer flexible schedules

Remember, the goal isn't to pile on as many volunteer hours or internships as possible. Instead, focus on quality experiences that genuinely interest you and align with your potential career paths. It's better to have a few meaningful experiences where you've learned and grown than a long list of superficial ones.

Let's talk about time management because I know what you're thinking - *"How am I supposed to fit this in with everything else?"* The key is to start small. Even dedicating just 2-3 hours a week to a volunteer position can provide valuable experience. Many organizations offer flexible scheduling specifically designed to work around school commitments. Virtual opportunities have made participating even easier without sacrificing your other responsibilities.

A critical aspect of both volunteering and internships is documentation.

Keep a detailed record of your experiences, including:

- Specific projects you worked on
- Skills you developed
- Achievements and outcomes
- People you worked with or learned from
- Challenges you overcame

This documentation will be invaluable when updating your resume, writing college applications, or interviewing for future opportunities. It's also a great way to reflect on your growth and identify areas where you'd like to gain more experience.

The connections you make through volunteering and internships can be just as valuable as the experience itself. These relationships can lead to mentorship opportunities, letters of recommendation, and even future job offers. Don't be shy about building professional relationships - most people are happy to help motivated young people who show genuine interest and dedication.

Remember, every experience is a learning opportunity, even if it helps you discover what you don't want to do. Maybe you'll volunteer at a veterinary clinic and realize you don't actually enjoy working with animals as much as you thought - that's valuable information! The goal is to explore, learn, and grow while building a foundation for your future career.

Global Perspective: Exchange Programs, Virtual International Experiences, and Cultural Competency

In today's interconnected world, having a global perspective isn't just a nice thing to have - it's becoming essential for career success. Whether you're planning to work for an international company, start your own global business, or simply want to be more competitive in your chosen field, understanding different cultures and developing international experience can give you a significant advantage.

I remember working with Lily, a student who felt limited by her inability to travel abroad due to family commitments. Together, we discovered that building a global experience doesn't always require a passport. Through virtual exchange programs, she connected with students from Japan, Brazil, and India, practicing her language skills and learning about business practices in different cultures. These experiences later helped her land an internship with a global marketing firm without leaving her hometown.

Let's explore some practical ways to gain international experience and develop cultural competency:

- Virtual exchange programs: connect with peers worldwide through structured online programs

- Language learning apps and cultural exchange platforms

- International online volunteering opportunities

- Virtual global internships with international organizations

- Cross-cultural project collaboration

The beauty of today's technology is that you can gain meaningful international experience without the expense of traditional study abroad programs. Virtual exchange programs, for instance, allow you to collaborate with peers from different countries on real projects, developing both cultural awareness and practical skills.

Cultural competency goes beyond just knowing about different cultures - it's about developing the ability to work effectively with people from diverse backgrounds. Employers increasingly value this skill, especially as remote work makes international collaboration more common. Think of cultural competency as a muscle that gets stronger with each cross-cultural interaction you have.

One effective way to develop cultural competency is through structured virtual international experiences.

These might include:

- Participating in global student forums
- Working on international group projects
- Taking part in virtual cultural exchange events
- Joining international youth leadership programs
- Contributing to global online communities

During my workshops, I often emphasize that building cultural competency isn't just about learning facts about different countries - it's about developing empathy, adaptability, and communication skills that work across cultures. These soft skills are invaluable in any career path, whether you're working locally or globally.

Here's a practical approach to building your global perspective:

- Start with research about different cultures and business practices
- Practice cross-cultural communication through online platforms
- Document your international experiences and learnings
- Build a network of international contacts
- Develop language skills through regular practice

Remember, even small steps toward building international experience can make a big difference in your career journey. Whether it's participating in a one-time virtual cultural exchange event or committing to a longer-term international project, each experience adds to your global perspective.

One of my students, Marcus, started by joining an international gaming community. He learned about different communication styles, time zone management, and cultural perspectives in this informal setting. These skills later proved invaluable when he started freelancing as a game developer, working with clients from around the world.

When documenting your international experiences for college applications or job interviews, focus on specific skills and insights you've gained. For example, instead of just mentioning that you participated in a virtual exchange program, highlight how it improved your cross-cultural communication skills or helped you understand different approaches to problem-solving.

The global perspective you develop now can open doors throughout your career. Many employers specifically look for candidates who can demonstrate cultural competency and international experience. In our increasingly connected world, these skills can set you apart whether you're applying for college, seeking internships, or starting your own business.

Remember, building a global perspective is an ongoing journey, not a destination. Each international interaction, whether virtual or in-person, adds to your understanding and capabilities. Start small, stay curious, and be open to learning from every cross-cultural experience you encounter.

Documenting Your Journey: Creating a Professional Portfolio and Experience Log

In today's digital world, keeping track of your experiences and achievements is more important than ever. Think of your professional portfolio as your personal highlight reel - it's where you showcase your best work, document your growth, and prove your capabilities to future employers or college admissions officers. But how do you create one that stands out?

I recently worked with Tyler, a creative 16-year-old who struggled to organize his various experiences and projects. He had done some amazing things - from coding a simple app to organizing a local gaming tournament - but when asked about his interview experience, he would freeze up or forget important details. Together, we developed a system for documenting his journey that made showcasing his achievements and tracking his growth easy.

Let's break down the essential elements of a strong professional portfolio:

- Digital portfolio platform (like LinkedIn, Behance, or a personal website)
- Project showcase (with clear descriptions and outcomes)
- Skills log (tracking both technical and soft skills)
- Experience timeline (documenting your growth)
- Achievements and certifications
- Testimonials or references

The key to creating an effective portfolio is starting early and updating it regularly. Don't wait until you're applying for college or jobs to begin documenting your experiences. Keep a simple log or journal where you record projects, volunteer work, and even small achievements as they happen. This will make it much easier to build your portfolio later and ensure you don't forget important details.

Here's a practical tip I share with all my students: create a "career journal" on your phone. Every time you complete a project, learn a new skill, or achieve something noteworthy, take a quick note with the date, what you did, and what you learned. Include photos or screenshots when possible. This simple habit can become a goldmine of information when building your portfolio or preparing for interviews.

One effective way to organize your experience log is by categories:

- Technical skills (coding languages learned, software mastered)
- Leadership experience (team projects, club leadership)
- Creative projects (art, writing, design work)
- Volunteer work (community service, mentoring)
- Academic achievements (relevant coursework, special projects)

Remember, your portfolio should tell a story about who you are and where you're headed. It's not just a list of things you've done—it's a narrative about your growth and potential. When documenting your experiences, focus on both what you did and what you learned from each opportunity.

For example, instead of just noting "volunteered at the local food bank", you might write: "coordinated food donations at Community Food Bank - developed inventory management skills, learned to use tracking software, and improved team communication while working with diverse volunteers".

In today's digital age, consider creating both a physical and digital portfolio.

Your digital portfolio might include:

- A personal website or blog
- LinkedIn profile
- GitHub account (for coding projects)
- Digital art portfolio
- Video demonstrations of skills

One of the most powerful aspects of maintaining a professional portfolio is that it helps you identify patterns in your interests and strengths. As you document your experiences, you might notice themes emerging that can guide your career choices. Maybe you'll see that you consistently enjoy leadership roles or that your best work involves creative problem-solving.

When it comes to organizing your experience log, consider using the **STAR method to document each significant experience:**

- Situation (What was the context?)
- Task (What needed to be done?)
- Action (What did you do?)
- Result (What was the outcome?)

This format helps you tell compelling stories about your experiences, making preparing for future interviews or applications easier. It also helps you reflect on what you've learned and how you've grown from each experience.

Don't forget to include evidence of your work whenever possible. This might mean screenshots of projects, photos of events you organized, links to published work, or certificates from courses you've completed. Real evidence makes your portfolio more credible and engaging.

Finally, remember that your portfolio is a living document that should grow and evolve with you. Set regular times (maybe once a month) to update your experience log and portfolio. Remove outdated information, add new achievements, and refine how you present your experiences. This ongoing maintenance ensures you're always ready to showcase your best self when opportunities arise.

Your portfolio and experience log aren't just tools for job hunting - they're resources for personal reflection and growth. By documenting your journey, you create a clear picture of where you've been and where you might want to go next. This self-awareness is invaluable as you navigate your career path and make decisions about your future. As we wrap up this chapter on building your experience bank, remember that every skill you develop, every project you complete, and every connection you make is a valuable deposit in your professional future. As Emma's journey from shy volunteer to confident leader showed us, real-world experience isn't just about padding your resume - it's about discovering who you are and what you're capable of achieving.

Through strategic volunteering, internships, and international experiences (even virtual ones!), you're not just collecting experiences - you're building a foundation for your future career. Whether you're documenting your journey in a digital portfolio like Tyler, gaining a global perspective through virtual exchange programs like Lily, or turning your volunteer work into paid opportunities like Carlos, each experience adds another tool to your professional toolkit.

The beauty of building your experience bank now is that you have the freedom to experiment, learn, and even make mistakes without the pressure of a full-time career. You can try different roles, explore various industries, and discover what truly excites you. Remember, it's not about the quantity of experiences you collect but the quality of learning and growth each opportunity provides.

Key Takeaways

As you move forward, keep these key takeaways in mind:

- Start small, but think strategically about the experiences you pursue

- Document your journey and reflect on what you learn along the way
- Build your global perspective, even if you can't travel internationally
- Focus on developing both technical and soft skills through real-world experiences
- Use every opportunity to build meaningful professional connections

Your experience bank is like a garden - it needs regular attention, strategic planning, and time to grow. Some experiences will bloom quickly, while others might take longer to show their value. The key is to keep planting seeds of opportunity and nurturing them with dedication and purpose.

As you close this chapter, take a moment to reflect on your own experience bank. What deposits have you already made? What areas would you like to develop further? Remember, every expert was once a beginner, and every successful career started with those first few experiences. Your journey to building a rich and diverse experience bank starts now - make every opportunity count!

In the next chapter, we'll explore how to fund your future without the stress, building on the foundation of experiences you've gathered to create sustainable career pathways. Your experience bank is just one part of your career journey, but it's an essential building block for whatever path you choose to pursue.

Chapter 6

Money Smart

Funding Your Future Without the Stress

Money matters can feel overwhelming, especially when you're planning your future career path and education, but understanding the basics of financial planning doesn't have to be complicated or stressful. Just like building a house starts with a solid foundation, creating your financial future begins with understanding some fundamental principles that will serve you throughout your career journey. It's time to take control of your financial future, and this chapter will show you exactly how. Whether you dream of college, trade school, or starting your own business, understanding how to fund your goals is crucial for turning those dreams into reality.

Think of your financial journey like building your favorite playlist - you need to choose the right tracks (funding sources) and arrange them in the best order (financial planning) to create the perfect mix for your future. Just like how streaming changed how we listen to music, the landscape of education funding and career financing has transformed dramatically in recent years, offering more options than ever before.

Let me share a story that perfectly illustrates this. In my career guidance practice, I worked with Mia, a talented high school junior who dreamed of becoming a veterinarian but was paralyzed by fears about the cost of veterinary school. Her family had limited resources, and she worried that her dream was financially out of reach. Together, we created a comprehensive financial strategy. We started by researching and applying for scholarships - not just the well-known ones but also local and specialized opportunities. Mia began working part-time at a local animal shelter, which not only provided income for her savings account but also valuable experience for her future career. She learned to budget her earnings, allocating portions for immediate needs, college savings, and an emergency fund. By her senior year, Mia had secured several scholarships, built a solid savings foundation, and understood how to approach student loans for the remaining cost responsibly. More importantly, she had developed money management skills that would serve her throughout her career. Today, she's in her second year of undergraduate studies on her path to veterinary school, managing her finances confidently and serving as a peer mentor to other students navigating their own financial journeys.

Mia's story shows us that with the right strategy and mindset, financial obstacles don't have to stand between you and your career goals. In this chapter, we'll explore practical ways to fund your education and career development without drowning in debt. We'll look at everything from scholarship-hunting strategies to clever budgeting techniques and even explore creative ways to build your financial foundation while still in high school.

Remember, being money-smart doesn't mean you need to become a financial expert overnight. It's about learning the basics, making informed decisions, and building healthy financial habits that will serve you throughout your career journey. Whether you're saving for college, planning to start a business, or looking to fund specialized training, this chapter will provide you with the tools and knowledge you need to make your career dreams financially possible.

Let's break down the money barriers together and create a solid financial foundation for your future success. After all, understanding how to fund your future isn't just about paying for education - it's about gaining the freedom to pursue a career that genuinely excites you.

Smart Education Funding: Scholarships, Grants, and Loan Navigation

Let's talk about one of the biggest questions on every teen's mind: *"How am I going to pay for my education?"* The good news is that you've got more options than you might think, and I'm going to break them down in a way that actually makes sense.

First up, let's talk about free money (yes, you read that right!). Scholarships and grants are basically free cash for your education - you don't have to pay them back. Think of them as your education's best friends. They come in all shapes and sizes, from academic achievements to special talents and even unique interests like left-handed students or people who love creating duck tape prom outfits (seriously, that's a real thing!).

Here's your scholarship-hunting strategy:

- Start local: Check with your school counselor, local businesses, and community organizations

- Use scholarship search engines wisely: Set up profiles on reputable sites and apply regularly

- Look for niche opportunities: Your hobbies, heritage, or specific skills might qualify you for specialized scholarships

- Track deadlines: Create a scholarship calendar to stay organized

Now, let's dive into grants. Unlike most scholarships, grants are usually need-based, meaning they look at your family's financial situation. The most common is the Federal Pell Grant, but there are tons of others out there. The key is to fill out your FAFSA (Free Application for Federal Student Aid) as early as possible. Mark October 1st on your calendar because that's when the application opens each year.

But what if scholarships and grants don't cover everything? That's where student loans come in. Now, I know loans can sound scary, but they're like tools - they're helpful when used wisely. Think of them as investing in your future self.

Here's your loan navigation guide:

- Always start with federal loans: They typically have better interest rates and more flexible repayment options

- Understand the difference between subsidized and unsubsidized loans

- Only borrow what you absolutely need - not what you're offered

- Research loan forgiveness programs for your intended career path

Let me share a quick success story from my career guidance practice. I worked with Carlos, who wanted to become an engineer but was worried about the cost. We created a "funding portfolio" approach like a financial puzzle where different pieces work together. He started by applying to 3-5 scholarships every week (treating it like a part-time job), secured several local grants, and only then considered loans to fill the gaps. By graduation, he had pieced together enough funding through a mix of sources to attend his dream school with minimal debt.

Here's a pro tip many teens miss: Look beyond just college funding. Many trade schools and certification programs have their own scholarship programs, and some employers offer tuition reimbursement or apprenticeship programs where you can earn while you learn.

Remember to think creatively about funding your education.

You could:

- Start at a community college to save money on core classes.

- Consider work-study programs or part-time jobs with tuition benefits.

- Look into dual enrollment programs while still in high school.

The key to smart education funding is starting early and casting a wide net. Don't put all your eggs in one basket - or, in this case, don't count on just one funding source. Mix and match different options to create a funding strategy that works for you.

And here's something many people don't talk about: it's okay to take a gap year to work and save money or to spread your education out over a more extended period while working part-time. No rule says you have to do everything at once or follow the traditional path.

The most important thing is to be proactive and start planning now. Create a spreadsheet to track scholarship applications, set up alerts for new opportunities, and don't be afraid to reach out to financial aid offices - they're there to help you navigate this process.

Remember Mia from earlier in this chapter? She made it work by combining multiple funding sources, and you can, too. The key is to start early, stay organized, and be persistent. Your future self will thank you for taking the time to explore all your options and make informed decisions about funding your education.

Building Your Financial Foundation: Budgeting and Saving Strategies

Let's talk about something that might sound boring but is actually your secret weapon for future success - budgeting and saving! I know it's not as exciting as TikTok trends, but trust me, this is the stuff that can make your dreams happen.

Think of budgeting like being the CEO of your own life - you're making decisions about where your money goes instead of wondering where it went. One of my favorite techniques to share with teens is the 50-30-20 rule but with a teen-friendly twist. Instead of the traditional adult breakdown, we'll adapt it to your situation: 50% for your future (savings and education), 30% for your needs (like phone bills or gas money), and 20% for fun stuff (because you're still young and should enjoy life!).

Here's your starter kit for building solid money habits:

- Track your spending for two weeks (yes, even those tiny snack purchases!)

- Set up separate savings accounts for different goals (think: college fund, car fund, emergency stash)

- Use money management apps designed for teens to make budgeting easier

- Look for ways to earn while learning (part-time jobs, online gigs, or selling items you create)

Let me share a story about one of my students, Taylor, who thought saving on her weekend job income was impossible. We started small - she began saving just $10 from each paycheck, then gradually increased it as she got comfortable budgeting. She used a simple notes app to track every dollar and started noticing patterns in her spending. The game-changer? She realized she was spending $15 a week on coffee shop drinks. By making coffee at home and bringing it in a thermos, she redirected that money to her savings. Within six months, she had saved enough for her first laptop - something she needed for her graphic design side hustle.

One of the biggest myths I hear from teens is, *"I don't make enough to save."* But here's the truth: it's not about how much you save. It's about building the habit. Even saving $5 a week adds up to $260 a year - that's a solid start! The key is consistency and starting early.

Here are some teen-specific saving strategies that actually work:

- Use the 24-hour rule before making any non-essential purchase

- Set up automatic savings transfers (even if it's just a few dollars)

- Find a savings buddy to keep you accountable

- Look for student discounts everywhere - they add up!

But let's get real - saving money isn't just about denying yourself everything fun. It's about making smart choices that align with your goals. Want to go to that concert next month? Great! Let's figure out how to save for it while keeping your other financial goals on track.

I always encourage teens to think about money in terms of time and value. Before buying something, ask yourself, 'How many hours of work did this cost me?' and 'Will this matter to me in a month?' This simple mental check can help you make better spending decisions.

Here's a power move that most teens don't know about: you can start building your credit history early (with parental supervision) by becoming an authorized user on a parent's credit card. This can give you a head start on building good credit, which will be super important when you're ready to rent an apartment or buy a car.

Remember, building your financial foundation isn't about becoming a money expert overnight. It's about developing healthy habits that will serve you throughout your career journey. Start small, stay consistent, and watch your savings grow.

One last pro tip: create a "money diary" where you write down your financial goals and track your progress. This isn't just about numbers - it's about understanding your relationship with money and building confidence in your financial decisions. When you can see your progress, even small wins feel huge!

The most important thing to remember is that everyone's financial journey is different. What works for your friends might not work for you, and that's totally okay. The goal is to find a system that fits your life and helps you reach your goals, whether saving for college, starting a business, or building your emergency fund.

Understanding Credit and Making Smart Money Choices

Let's talk about something that might seem a bit intimidating but is super important for your future - credit and smart money choices. Think of credit like your financial reputation - a report card showing how well you handle money and pay your bills. And just like your social media presence can impact your life, your credit score can affect everything from renting your first apartment to landing your dream job.

I remember working with Jasmine, a senior in high school who was confused about why credit mattered since she didn't have any credit cards. Together, we explored how credit would impact her future goals - from getting her own phone plan to eventually starting her own business. She learned that building good credit is like planting a tree - the sooner you start, the stronger it grows.

Here are some key things every teen should know about credit:

- Your credit score is like a financial GPA - it ranges from 300 to 850, and higher is better

- Credit reports track how you handle money and pay bills

- Future employers and landlords might check your credit

- Building good credit takes time, but damaging it can happen quickly

Now, you might be thinking, *"But I'm too young for credit cards!"*

Actually, there are several ways to start building credit responsibly as a teen:

- Become an authorized user on a parent's credit card (if they have good credit)

- Start with a secured credit card when you're old enough

- Make sure your name is on some utility bills if you're working

Let me share another story from my practice. I worked with Marcus, who wanted to start building credit but was worried about falling into debt like his older sister. We created a "credit training wheels" plan: He became an authorized user on his mom's card but only used it for gas once a month, paying it off immediately. This helped him build credit while developing responsible habits.

Here's your smart money choices starter pack:

- Always pay bills on time - set reminders on your phone if needed

- Keep your spending well below your limits

- Check your credit report regularly (it's free!)

- Never share personal financial information online

One of the biggest myths I hear from teens is that they need to carry a balance on credit cards to build credit. That's totally false! You can build excellent credit by using your card responsibly and paying it off in full each month. In fact, carrying a balance just means you're paying extra money in interest.

Think of credit as a powerful tool - it can help you build your future or cause serious damage, depending on how you use it. Just like you wouldn't jump into driving a car without learning the rules of the road, don't jump into using credit without understanding how it works.

Here are some warning signs that you might be heading for credit trouble:

- Using credit for everyday purchases, you can't afford
- Making only minimum payments
- Applying for multiple credit cards at once
- Letting others borrow your card

Remember, your credit journey is a marathon, not a sprint. Start slow, stay informed, and make decisions for which your future self will thank you. Whether you are planning to go to college, start a business, or jump straight into your career, good credit will make that journey easier.

One final pro tip: create a "credit and bills" calendar. Mark when payments are due and set up automatic payments if possible. This simple habit can save you from late fees and credit score damage. Your future self will thank you for starting these good habits now when the stakes are lower.

And here's something many teens don't realize - you can start practicing good credit habits even before you have any credit accounts. Keep track of your spending, pay your phone bill on time, and save receipts. These habits will make the transition to managing credit much easier when the time comes.

Remember, building good credit is part of your overall financial health. It's not about trying to game the system or finding shortcuts - it's about demonstrating that you can handle money responsibly over time. This foundation will give you more options and opportunities as you move forward in your career journey. As we wrap up this chapter on smart money management, let's take a moment to reflect on the key strategies we've explored to fund your future without stress. Remember Mia's journey? Her story shows us that with the right approach, financial obstacles don't have to stand between you and your dreams.

Through this chapter, we've discovered that building a solid financial foundation isn't just about having money - it's about making smart choices and developing healthy money habits early on. We've explored multiple paths to funding your education, from scholarships and grants to responsible student loan management. We've learned that building good credit isn't about fancy financial tricks but about consistent, responsible choices that add up over time.

The financial strategies we've discussed - like the teen-friendly 50-30-20 rule, smart scholarship hunting, and credit-building basics - are tools you can start using right now to build your future. Whether you're planning for college, trade school, or entrepreneurship, understanding these financial fundamentals gives you the power to make informed decisions about your career path.

But here's the real talk - money management isn't just about spreadsheets and savings accounts. It's about creating freedom and options for your future self. Every smart financial choice you make today opens up more possibilities tomorrow. Maybe you'll want to start your own business, travel while working remotely, or pursue advanced education - good financial habits make all these paths possible.

Remember Taylor's coffee shop revelation? Sometimes, the slightest changes in how we handle money can lead to big results. You don't need to transform your financial life overnight. Start small, stay consistent, and watch your financial confidence grow alongside your savings.

As you move forward, keep this in mind: your financial journey is unique to you. While your friends might make different choices, finding a system that works for your goals and situation matters. Whether saving for college, building an emergency fund, or funding your first business venture, the financial foundations you build now will support you throughout your career journey.

So take that first step. Maybe it's tracking your spending for a week, researching scholarship opportunities, or having an honest conversation with your parents about college funding. Whatever it is, start today. Your future self will thank you for the financial wisdom and healthy money habits you're developing right now.

Remember, being money-smart isn't about having perfect finances - it's about making informed choices that align with your goals and values. As you continue your career exploration journey, carry these financial tools with you. They'll help you turn your career dreams into reality, one smart money choice at a time.

Chapter 7

The Multi-Passionate Path

Creating Your Portfolio Career

In today's dynamic job market, you don't have to choose just one career path - you can create a unique professional journey that embraces all your passions and talents. Welcome to the world of portfolio careers, where being multi-passionate isn't a disadvantage but rather a superpower that can lead to both personal fulfillment and financial success. More than ever before, today's workforce is embracing the idea that success doesn't have to mean choosing just one career path. Think of your career journey as creating a unique playlist - you can mix different songs (or, in this case, jobs and skills) that work harmoniously together to create something that's uniquely you. This approach to building a career is gaining popularity, especially among Gen Z, who are likelier to pursue multiple income streams rather than stick to traditional nine-to-five jobs.

I've seen firsthand how embracing multiple passions can lead to incredible opportunities. Take Olivia, a creative 17-year-old who came to me feeling torn between her love for music, her talent for graphic design, and her interest in teaching. Rather than forcing her to choose one path, we explored how she could build a portfolio career that incorporated all three passions. She started by offering graphic design services to local music venues while teaching basic music theory to elementary students after school. As her skills grew, she expanded into creating visual branding for musicians and designing educational materials for music teachers. Within two years, Olivia had built a sustainable portfolio career that allowed her to engage with all her interests. She now splits her time between teaching music part-time at a local arts center, freelancing as a graphic designer for entertainment clients, and performing at weekend events. Her story demonstrates how embracing multiple passions can lead to a unique and fulfilling career path that defies traditional boundaries.

Building a portfolio career isn't just about following multiple interests - it's also a smart strategy in today's rapidly changing job market. By developing diverse skills and income streams, you create a safety net that can protect you from economic uncertainties while giving you the freedom to explore new opportunities as they arise. Throughout this chapter, we'll explore how you can identify your interests, develop complementary skills, and weave them together into a career that's as unique as yours.

We'll dive into practical strategies for managing multiple professional pursuits, from time management to personal branding. You'll learn how to present your diverse skill set to potential clients or employers and how to create synergies between different aspects of your work life. Most importantly, you'll discover that being multi-passionate isn't a weakness to overcome - it's a strength to embrace and leverage for career success.

Building Multiple Income Streams: Combining Part-time Work, Freelancing, and Side Hustles

Let's talk about one of the coolest trends in today's work world - building multiple income streams! Think of it like being a DJ who knows how to mix different tracks to create an awesome playlist. Instead of relying on just one source of income, you can blend different types of work to create a stable and exciting career that fits your lifestyle.

One of my favorite success stories is about Jasmine, a student I worked with who turned her love for social media and fitness into a thriving combination of income streams. She started by working part-time at a local gym (steady income ✓), then began offering online workout tips through her social media (side hustle ✓), and eventually launched a small business selling workout planners she designed herself (entrepreneurship ✓). The best part? She did all this while still in high school!

Here are some popular ways to build multiple income streams:

- Part-time work: Traditional jobs that provide steady income and valuable experience

- Freelancing: Using your skills to work on projects for different clients

- Digital side hustles: Content creation, social media management, or online tutoring

- Small business ventures: Selling products or services, either online or locally

- Skill-based gigs: Teaching, coaching, or sharing your expertise

The key to making this work is starting small and building gradually. You don't need to juggle everything at once! Begin with one reliable income source, like a part-time job, then experiment with side projects that interest you. This approach gives you the security of regular income while you explore other opportunities.

One of the most significant advantages of building multiple income streams is the flexibility it offers. You can scale your different activities up or down depending on your schedule, school commitments, or changing interests. Plus, having diverse income sources provides financial security - if one stream slows down, you've got others to fall back on.

Time management becomes super important when you're juggling different income streams. I always recommend using the "time blocking" technique to my students. Break your day into chunks dedicated to specific activities. For example, you might work your part-time job after school, spend Saturday mornings on your freelance projects, and dedicate Sunday afternoons to developing your side business.

Here's a pro tip: Look for ways your different income streams can complement each other. Maybe your part-time job gives you skills you can use in your freelance work, or your side hustle teaches you business skills that make you more valuable at your regular job. It's all about finding those sweet spots where your different activities create positive feedback loops.

Remember to start with activities that align with your current skills and interests. If you're tech-savvy, consider combining a part-time job in retail with freelance web design. Love sports? You might pair coaching youth teams with creating sports content for social media. The possibilities are endless!

It's also important to understand that building multiple income streams isn't about working 24/7. It's about being smart with your time and energy. Focus on activities that give you the best return for your effort, and don't be afraid to drop things that aren't working. Your goal should be creating a sustainable mix of income sources that energizes rather than exhausts you.

As you explore different income streams, keep detailed records of what works and what doesn't. Track your earnings, time investment, and, most importantly, how each activity makes you feel. This information will help you make better decisions about where to focus your energy as you build your portfolio career.

The beauty of this approach is that it allows you to test different career paths without committing fully to any single one. You might discover that what you thought would be a side hustle actually has the potential to become your primary career or that combining several part-time roles gives you more satisfaction than a traditional full-time job would.

Time Management and Work-Life Integration for Multi-Passionate Professionals

Managing your time when juggling multiple passions and projects isn't just about cramming more stuff into your day - it's about creating a lifestyle that feels energizing rather than exhausting. I've seen too many multi-passionate teens burn out trying to do everything at once, which is why learning to balance your various interests is super important.

Let me share a story about Riley, a student I worked with who was trying to balance her photography business, coding projects, and school responsibilities. At first, she was constantly stressed, staying up late to edit photos and missing deadlines for her coding work. Together, we developed a system that helped her thrive instead of just surviving.

Here are some game-changing strategies for managing multiple pursuits:

- Energy mapping: Track when you're most creative, focused, or energetic and schedule tasks accordingly

- Theme days: Dedicate specific days to different projects (like "Marketing Mondays" or "Creative Thursdays")

- Buffer zones: Build in transition time between activities to avoid mental overload

- Digital boundaries: Set specific times for checking emails and social media to avoid constant interruptions

One of the biggest myths about work-life integration is that you need perfect balance daily. That's like expecting the weather to be exactly the same all year round - it's just not realistic! Instead, think about balance over longer periods, like weeks or months. Some weeks, you might focus more on one project, while others require attention to different areas of your life.

The key to successful work-life integration is understanding that "work" and "life" aren't opposing forces - they're parts of the same whole. When pursuing activities you're passionate about, the line between work and play often blurs in the best possible way. It's about creating synergies between different areas of your life rather than keeping them strictly separated.

Here's a practical tip I always share with my students: use the "energy bucket" system. Imagine you have three buckets - one for high-energy tasks, one for medium-energy tasks, and one for low-energy tasks. When feeling super motivated and focused, tackle things from your high-energy bucket. When you're in a more relaxed state, work on low-energy tasks. This approach helps you stay productive without burning out.

Technology can be both a blessing and a curse when managing multiple pursuits. While it's tempting to use every productivity app out there, I recommend starting with just one or two tools that really work for you. A simple calendar app and a task management tool are usually enough to keep track of your various commitments without getting overwhelmed by the tools themselves.

Remember, it's totally okay to adjust your commitments as needed. Being multi-passionate doesn't mean you have to actively pursue all your interests at the same intensity all the time. Sometimes certain projects or activities might need to take a back seat while you focus on others. This isn't giving up - it's being strategic about your energy and time.

One of the most valuable skills you can develop is recognizing when you need to step back and recharge. Schedule regular "me time" just like you would any other important appointment. This isn't selfish - it's about maintaining the energy you need to pursue all your passions effectively.

Finally, don't forget to celebrate your wins, no matter how small they seem. Successfully juggling multiple interests is a skill that takes time to develop. Each time you complete a project, meet a deadline or find a better way to manage your time, you build valuable experience that will serve you throughout your career journey.

Creating a Unified Personal Brand Across Different Professional Roles

When you're rocking multiple roles in your career life, creating a personal brand that ties everything together is like being the director of your own fantastic movie. Every scene might be different, but they all tell one compelling story about you. I've helped many teens navigate this challenge, and one of my favorite success stories is about Marcus, a student who combined his passion for skateboarding, graphic design, and teaching into one cohesive brand.

Marcus initially worried that his diverse interests would seem scattered to potential clients and employers. Together, we worked on developing what I call a "brand bridge" - finding the common themes that connect all his pursuits. He realized that creativity and youth culture were the threads that tied everything together. Now, his personal brand focuses on "inspiring youth through creative expression", whether he teaches skateboarding, designing logos for local businesses, or creating social media content.

Here are some key strategies for building your unified personal brand:

- Find your core message: Identify the values and themes that appear across all your interests

- Create a consistent visual identity: Use similar colors, fonts, and styles across all platforms

- Develop your brand story: Craft a narrative that explains how your different roles complement each other

- Choose platforms wisely: Select social media and professional platforms that best showcase your various skills

Think of your personal brand like your favorite playlist - each song might be different, but they all reflect your unique taste and style. When presenting yourself online or in person, focus on how your different roles complement each other rather than trying to keep them completely separate.

One common mistake I see teens make is thinking they need to create separate personas for each of their professional roles. Instead, embrace how your different interests and skills make you unique. For example, if you're both a coder and a musician, you might highlight how both roles require creativity, pattern recognition, and attention to detail.

Your digital presence is super important when building a unified brand. Consider creating a personal website showcasing all your roles while highlighting their connections. This becomes your digital home base - a place where people can see the full picture of who you are professionally.

Here's a pro tip:

Create what I call a "brand map" - a simple document that outlines:

- Your core values and mission

- Key skills that overlap between your different roles

- The unique value you bring to each area

- How do your different roles support and enhance each other

Remember, authenticity is key when building your personal brand. Don't try to force connections that aren't there or pretend to be someone you're not. Instead, focus on genuinely communicating how your diverse interests and skills make you uniquely qualified to solve specific problems or meet particular needs.

When it comes to social media, you don't need separate accounts for every role. Instead, create content that shows how your different interests intersect. For instance, if you're into both photography and environmental activism, your Instagram might feature stunning nature photos alongside captions about conservation.

Networking becomes especially interesting when you have multiple professional roles. You might find that connections from one area of your work can lead to opportunities in another. Always be open about your various interests - you never know when someone might need exactly your unique combination of skills.

Finally, don't forget that your personal brand will evolve as you grow and discover new interests. It's okay to update and refine your brand over time. The key is maintaining enough consistency that people understand who you are and what you stand for while allowing room for growth and new directions.

Your unified personal brand should feel like a natural extension of who you are, not a carefully constructed facade. When done right, it helps others understand and appreciate the unique value you bring through your diverse skills and interests. Remember, in today's interconnected world, being multi-talented isn't a liability - it's a superpower that sets you apart from the crowd.

As we wrap up this chapter on multi-passionate careers, I hope you're feeling excited about the possibilities of creating a career path that's as unique as you are. Throughout our exploration of portfolio careers, we've seen how combining different interests and skills isn't just possible - it's becoming increasingly common and valuable in today's job market.

Olivia's story of blending music, graphic design, and teaching shows that success doesn't mean choosing just one path. Instead, it's about finding creative ways to weave your various passions into a fulfilling career tapestry. Remember how she started small, offering graphic design services to music venues while teaching on the side? That's the beauty of portfolio careers - you can start building them piece by piece, testing what works and adjusting as you go.

We've covered essential strategies for juggling multiple roles, from time management techniques like energy mapping to creating a unified personal brand that tells your unique story. These skills aren't just about managing various jobs - they're about creating a sustainable lifestyle that lets you pursue all your interests while maintaining balance and avoiding burnout.

As you move forward, remember that being multi-passionate isn't a weakness to overcome - it's a strength to embrace. In a world where jobs and industries constantly evolve, diverse skills and interests can make you more adaptable and resilient. Whether you're interested in combining traditional employment with freelance work, starting your own business while maintaining a part-time job, or creating your own unique combination of roles, there's a way to make it work.

Key Takeaway

The key takeaway from this chapter isn't just that portfolio careers are possible and can be incredibly rewarding when approached thoughtfully and strategically. You can create a professionally fulfilling and personally satisfying career by understanding how to manage your time, integrate different aspects of your work life, and present your diverse skills cohesively.

As you continue your career journey, keep experimenting with different combinations of work and interests. Don't be afraid to adjust your approach as you learn what works best for you. Remember, the goal isn't to do everything at once but to create a sustainable mix of activities that energizes rather than exhausts you.

Your portfolio career might look different from everyone else's - and that's exactly how it should be. Whether you're combining coding with content creation, mixing art with entrepreneurship, or blending teaching with technology, your unique combination of skills and interests is what will set you apart in today's job market.

Take these strategies, tools, and insights and use them to start building your own multi-passionate career path. Remember, you don't have to have it all figured out right now. Start small, experiment, and keep refining your approach as you grow. Your future career isn't about fitting into a predetermined box - it's about creating your own unique path that celebrates who you are and what you love to do.

Chapter 8

BUILDING YOUR BRAND

Networking and Personal Marketing in the Digital Age

Your personal brand is like a digital fingerprint that tells the world who you are professionally, what you stand for, and what unique value you bring to the table. In today's interconnected world, building and maintaining this brand isn't optional - it's an essential part of career development that begins long before you land your first job. In this digital age, your online presence can open doors to opportunities you never imagined possible. Whether you're sharing your artwork on Instagram, building connections on LinkedIn, or showcasing your coding projects on GitHub, every digital footprint you leave contributes to how the world perceives you professionally.

Think of your personal brand as your professional story. It's not just about what you do but how you present your unique combination of skills, interests, and values to the world. It's about authentically communicating who you are and what you stand for in a way that resonates with others.

During a career workshop I conducted for high school students, I met David, a talented 16-year-old photographer who struggled to showcase his work professionally. While he had impressive skills, his online presence consisted mainly of random social media posts that didn't reflect his aspirations. Together, we worked on developing his personal brand strategy. We created a professional portfolio website, established a business-focused Instagram account separate from his personal one, and developed a LinkedIn profile highlighting his growing expertise in photography. David learned to network by joining online photography communities and attending local arts events. He started documenting school events, offering classmates headshots, and building their professional profiles. Within six months, his structured approach to personal branding led to several paid photography opportunities and an internship with a local marketing agency. His story demonstrates how thoughtful personal branding and networking can open doors even for young professionals just starting their journey.

Building your brand isn't about creating a perfect, polished version of yourself - it's about being authentic while presenting yourself professionally. It's about finding that sweet spot between being relatable and being professional, between showing your personality and maintaining appropriate boundaries.

In this chapter, we'll explore how to create and maintain a strong personal brand that grows with you, how to network effectively both online and offline, and how to use digital tools to showcase your skills and achievements. You'll learn practical strategies for managing your digital presence, building meaningful professional relationships, and creating a personal marketing toolkit that will serve you throughout your career journey.

Digital Presence Management: Creating and Maintaining Your Professional Online Identity

Let's talk about managing your digital presence - it's basically like curating your own personal brand online. Think of it as your digital first impression. Just like you wouldn't show up for a job interview in your pajamas, you need to make sure your online presence shows your best professional self.

The first step in managing your digital presence is thoroughly auditing your current online footprint. Open up your favorite search engine and type in your name. What comes up? Are there any old social media posts or photos that might make a future employer raise an eyebrow? Remember, colleges and employers often check social media profiles during their selection process.

Here are some key elements to focus on when building your professional online presence:

- Choose professional usernames and handles across platforms

- Use a clear, professional photo for your profiles

- Create separate personal and professional accounts where needed

- Regularly review and update your privacy settings

- Be mindful of what you like, share, and comment on

One of my students, Jasmine, learned this lesson the hard way when she applied for a competitive internship. Although she had excellent grades and impressive volunteer experience, she hadn't considered her social media presence. During her interview, the employer mentioned seeing some of her TikTok dance challenges - not exactly the professional image Jasmine was hoping to project! Together, we worked on creating separate personal and professional accounts, and she learned to be more mindful of what she posted publicly.

When it comes to building a positive digital presence, consistency is key. Your LinkedIn profile should align with your professional Instagram feed and your personal website (if you have one). Think of it as telling your professional story across different platforms. Each platform can highlight various aspects of your skills and personality, but they should all paint a cohesive picture of who you are professionally.

Here are some platform-specific tips to consider:

- LinkedIn: Keep your profile updated, join relevant groups, and share industry-related content

- Instagram: Consider a separate professional account to showcase your work or interests

- Twitter: Follow industry leaders and engage in professional conversations

- Personal Website/Portfolio: Showcase your best work and keep it current

Remember, your digital presence isn't just about avoiding harmful content - it's about actively creating positive content that showcases your skills, interests, and professional growth. Share your achievements, write about topics in your field of interest, or create content demonstrating your expertise.

One effective strategy is to document your learning journey. Are you learning to code? Share your progress and projects. Interested in photography? Post your best shots with thoughtful captions about your creative process. This not only helps build your professional presence but also connects you with others in your field of interest.

Managing your digital presence might seem overwhelming at first, but think of it as an ongoing project rather than a one-time task. Set aside some time each month to review and update your profiles, create new content, and ensure your online presence continues to reflect your growing skills and evolving career goals.

Here's a monthly digital presence checklist to get you started:

- Review your privacy settings across all platforms
- Update your profiles with any new skills or achievements
- Create and share relevant content in your field of interest
- Engage with your professional network
- Google yourself to monitor your online presence

Remember, your digital presence is a powerful tool for building your future career. Used wisely, it can open doors to opportunities, connect you with mentors, and help you stand out in a competitive job market. The key is to be intentional about what you share and consistently maintain your professional image across all platforms.

As you build your digital presence, always keep in mind that the internet has a long memory. Before posting anything, ask yourself: "Would I be comfortable with a future employer seeing this?" If the answer is no, it's probably best to keep it private or not post it at all. Your digital presence should be authentic to who you are while still maintaining professional boundaries.

Strategic Networking: Building Authentic Professional Relationships Online and Offline

Building authentic professional relationships is like planting a garden - it takes time, care, and patience, but the results can be excellent. Whether you're connecting with people online or in person, the key is to focus on creating genuine connections rather than just collecting contacts. Let me share a story that perfectly illustrates this point.

One of my students, Tyler, was passionate about environmental science but didn't know anyone in the field. Instead of randomly sending connection requests on LinkedIn, we developed a strategy. He started by joining environmental clubs at school and volunteering at local conservation events. Online, he followed environmental scientists and organizations on social media, thoughtfully commenting on their posts and sharing his own experiences from his volunteer work. Within a few months, he built meaningful relationships with both local environmentalists and online connections who shared his interests.

Here are some key strategies for building authentic professional relationships:

- Start with your existing network (family, teachers, coaches)
- Join clubs and organizations related to your interests
- Attend local events in your field of interest
- Engage meaningfully on professional social media platforms
- Volunteer or intern to meet people in your chosen field

Remember, networking isn't about asking for favors - it's about building mutually beneficial relationships. Think about what you can offer others, even as a teenager. Maybe you're great with social media and could help a local business improve its online presence, or perhaps your tech skills could benefit a community organization.

When it comes to online networking, platforms like LinkedIn can seem intimidating at first. The key is to be authentic and professional. Your profile should tell your story - not just what you've done, but what you're passionate about and working toward. Share your projects, volunteer work, and learning experiences. Comment thoughtfully on posts that interest you, and don't be afraid to reach out to people with genuine questions or insights.

For offline networking, start with these approachable steps:

- Participate in school clubs related to your interests
- Attend career fairs and industry events in your area
- Get involved in community service projects
- Join local youth organizations or professional groups that welcome students
- Take part in workshops or classes in your field of interest

One effective strategy I've seen work well is what I call the "learning conversation" approach. Instead of asking for a job or internship, reach out to professionals with genuine curiosity about their work. Most people love sharing their experiences and insights with interested young people.

For example, another student of mine, Maria, was interested in graphic design. She started following local designers on Instagram and would ask thoughtful questions about their creative process. This led to several informal coffee chats where Maria learned about the industry and eventually secured a summer internship. The key was that she focused on learning and building relationships rather than immediately asking for opportunities.

When networking, whether online or offline, remember these essential principles:

- Be authentic and genuine in your interactions
- Show interest in others' work and experiences
- Follow up and maintain connections
- Express gratitude when others help you
- Share your own learning and experiences

Networking might feel awkward at first, but think of it as making professional friends. Just like you wouldn't immediately ask a new friend for a huge favor, naturally, take time to build professional relationships. Share your interests, ask questions, and look for ways to help others.

Here's a practical tip for maintaining your network: Create a simple system to track your connections. Note where you met them, what you discussed, and any follow-up actions. This could be as simple as using the notes section on your phone or creating a spreadsheet.

Remember that everyone you meet is potentially part of your professional network. That person sitting next to you in class might become a business partner in the future, or your volunteer supervisor might know someone in your dream company. Treat every interaction as an opportunity to learn and grow your network.

The most successful networkers approach networking with a genuine desire to learn and connect with others. They understand that networking is not about collecting business cards or LinkedIn connections—it's about building genuine relationships that can grow and evolve throughout their career journeys.

As you build your network, stay patient and persistent. Not every connection will lead to an opportunity, and that's okay. Focus on creating authentic relationships; professional opportunities will often follow naturally. Remember Tyler from earlier? His genuine interest in environmental science and consistent engagement led to a summer research assistant position with a local environmental organization - an opportunity that came through one of the connections he made while volunteering.

Personal Marketing Tools: From LinkedIn Profiles to Digital Portfolios

In today's digital world, having strong personal marketing tools is like having a professional superhero costume - they help you stand out and showcase your unique powers! Let's dive into the essential tools you'll need in your personal marketing toolkit to make a strong impression in your career journey.

LinkedIn might seem like a platform for "grown-ups", but creating a profile early can give you a huge advantage. Think of LinkedIn as your professional social media - it's where future employers, mentors, and colleagues will look to learn more about you. When I worked with Sophia, a 16-year-old aspiring web developer, she hesitated to join LinkedIn. *"Isn't it just for people with jobs?"* she asked. Together, we created a profile highlighting her coding projects, online courses, and volunteer work at her school's tech help desk. Within months, she connected with local tech professionals who offered guidance, eventually leading to an internship opportunity.

Here are the key elements of a strong LinkedIn profile for teens:

- A professional headshot (it doesn't need to be fancy - just clear and appropriate)

- A compelling headline that reflects your interests and aspirations

- A summary that tells your story and highlights your goals

- Sections for volunteer work, projects, and courses

- Skills and endorsements from teachers or mentors

Beyond LinkedIn, digital portfolios are becoming increasingly important, even for teens. Whether you're interested in art, writing, coding, or business, having a place to showcase your work can set you apart. Think of your digital portfolio as your professional highlight reel - it should feature your best work and demonstrate your growth over time.

I remember working with Marcus, who loved creating short videos but didn't know how to present his work professionally. We set up a simple website using a free platform where he could showcase his video projects, including school assignments and personal creative work. This portfolio helped him land a part-time job creating social media content for a local business while still in high school.

Here are some platforms to consider for your digital portfolio:

- Wix or WordPress for general portfolios
- GitHub for coding projects
- Behance for design work
- Medium for writing samples
- YouTube or Vimeo for video content

When creating your portfolio, remember these key principles:

- Keep it organized and easy to navigate
- Include brief descriptions of each project
- Highlight your role in group projects
- Update regularly with new work
- Include your contact information and social media links

Another essential personal marketing tool is your professional email address. While 'sparkleprincess@email.com' might have been cute when you were twelve, it's time for something more professional. Create an email address using some combination of your name - it's what you'll use for job applications, professional correspondence, and networking.

Resume building is also crucial, even if you haven't had a traditional job yet. Your resume should highlight your skills, experiences, and achievements in a clear, professional format. Include relevant coursework, volunteer work, projects, and any leadership roles in school clubs or organizations.

Here's a quick checklist for teen resume essentials:

- Contact information and professional email
- Education section with relevant coursework
- Skills section highlighting both technical and soft skills
- Experience section, including volunteer work and projects
- Activities and leadership roles
- Awards and achievements

Remember to tailor your personal marketing tools to your specific goals. If you're interested in creative fields, your portfolio might be more important than your LinkedIn profile. LinkedIn and GitHub might be your primary focus if you're pursuing business or technology.

One often overlooked but powerful personal marketing tool is the elevator pitch - a brief, compelling description of who you are and what interests you. Practice introducing yourself professionally in 30 seconds or less. This can be useful at career fairs, networking events, or even when meeting new people who could become part of your professional network.

As you build your personal marketing toolkit, remember that authenticity is key. These tools should reflect who you really are while presenting you in the most professional light possible. Start building these elements now, even if you think it's too early. The sooner you begin, the more time you have to refine and improve them.

Keep in mind that your personal marketing tools should grow and evolve with you. What you create today isn't set in stone. Regularly update your profiles, portfolios, and resumes to reflect new skills, experiences, and achievements. Think of them as living documents that tell the ongoing story of your professional journey.

Most importantly, maintain consistency across all your personal marketing tools. Your LinkedIn profile, digital portfolio, resume, and elevator pitch should tell the same story about who you are and what you're working towards. This consistency helps build a strong, recognizable personal brand that will serve you well throughout your career journey. As we wrap up this chapter on building your professional brand and presence, remember that your digital footprint is like your professional shadow - it follows you everywhere and can either work for you or against you. The key is taking control of that shadow and shaping it to reflect your best self.

Think back to David's story, how he transformed his scattered social media presence into a powerful professional portfolio that opened doors to real opportunities. Your journey might look different, but the principles remain the same: be authentic, professional, and strategic about presenting yourself to the world.

Whether you're building your LinkedIn profile, creating a digital portfolio, or networking at local events, remember that you're not just collecting followers or connections - you're building relationships that could shape your future career. Every post you share, every comment you make, and every person you connect with becomes part of your professional story.

Key Takeaways

Let's recap some key takeaways from this chapter:

- Your personal brand is more than just social media - it's the total package of how you present yourself professionally

- Authentic networking is about building genuine relationships, not just collecting contacts

- Your digital presence should evolve with you, reflecting your growing skills and experiences

- Professional marketing tools like LinkedIn and digital portfolios are essential, even for a teenager

- Managing your online presence is an ongoing process, not a one-time task

As you move forward in your career journey, think of your personal brand as a garden that needs regular tending. Some days, you'll plant new seeds (make new connections). On other days, you'll do maintenance (update your profiles), and sometimes, you'll need to prune (clean up old posts that no longer reflect who you are professionally).

Remember Jasmine's story about her TikTok videos being discovered during a job interview? It's a powerful reminder that the lines between personal and professional life can blur quickly in today's digital world.

But this isn't about being perfect - it's about being intentional about your online presence and professional relationships.

You don't need to have it all figured out right now. Start small, be consistent, and let your professional presence grow naturally alongside your skills and experiences. Whether you're interested in traditional careers, entrepreneurship, or creating your own unique path, a strong personal brand will be one of your most valuable assets.

In the next chapter, we'll explore navigating career conversations with family members and overcoming self-doubt - essential skills for building your professional presence. Remember, your personal brand isn't just about how others see you - it's about how you see yourself and the professional future you want to create.

Keep building, keep learning, and most importantly, stay true to yourself while presenting your best professional self to the world. Your future self will thank you for the foundations you're laying today.

Chapter 9

Family Dynamics

Navigating Career Conversations with Parents and Overcoming Self-Doubt

The conversation about your career choices with family members, especially parents, can feel like navigating through a maze of expectations, dreams, and sometimes conflicting values. While parents generally want the best for their children, their vision of "best" might not always align with your personal career aspirations and goals. When it comes to discussing career choices with parents, emotions can run high as both sides navigate differing perspectives, generational gaps, and cultural expectations. This chapter will help you develop strategies for effectively communicating your career aspirations while maintaining strong family relationships and building self-confidence.

Parental expectations often stem from a place of love and concern, but they can sometimes feel overwhelming or restrictive. Maybe you're passionate about digital art, but your parents insist on a "more stable" career in accounting. Or perhaps, like many teens, you're interested in emerging fields like AI development or social media management that your parents might not fully understand.

I've seen countless students struggle with this delicate balance in my career guidance practice. Take Maya's story, for example. As a talented 17-year-old, Maya dreamed of pursuing a career in environmental science but faced strong opposition from her parents, who wanted her to follow the family tradition of becoming a doctor. Maya's self-doubt grew as she struggled to honor her family's wishes and follow her passion. Through our sessions, we developed a strategy for Maya to research and present to her parents the growing importance of environmental science careers, including salary potential and job growth statistics. We also worked on building her confidence through small wins, like successfully leading an environmental project at her school. The turning point came when Maya organized a family meeting where she presented her well-researched career plan, addressing her parents' concerns about financial stability and professional growth. While initially skeptical, her parents began to see her passion and the viability of her chosen path.

Maya's experience highlights a common challenge many teens face: balancing personal career aspirations with family expectations while managing their own self-doubt. Throughout this chapter, we'll explore practical strategies for having productive career conversations with your parents, techniques for building self-confidence, and methods for addressing common concerns about career choices. You'll learn how to present your career plans effectively, manage cultural and generational differences, and maintain healthy family relationships during your career planning journey.

Remember, feeling uncertain or experiencing self-doubt during this process is completely normal. What matters is developing the tools and confidence to navigate these challenging conversations while staying true to your authentic career aspirations. Whether you're dealing with cultural expectations, generational differences, or simply different perspectives on what success looks like, this chapter will help you find your voice and build the confidence to advocate for your career choices.

Effective Communication Strategies: Having Productive Career Discussions with Parents

Having productive career discussions with your parents starts with understanding that effective communication is a two-way street. Let's explore some practical strategies to help you express your career aspirations while constructively addressing your parents' concerns.

One of the most powerful approaches is the "research first, talk later" method. Before initiating a serious career discussion with your parents, take time to gather solid information about your chosen career path. This means researching potential salaries, job growth projections, and real-world examples of successful people in your field of interest. When you come prepared with facts and data, you show your parents you're taking a thoughtful, mature approach to your career planning.

- Choose the right time and place for meaningful conversations

- Use "I feel" statements to express your thoughts without being confrontational

- Listen actively to your parents' concerns and acknowledge their perspective

- Come prepared with research about your chosen career path

- Share specific examples of how you plan to achieve your goals

Remember that timing is everything in these conversations. Avoid discussing career issues during stressful times or when either you or your parents are tired or distracted. Instead, consider scheduling a specific time to talk, perhaps over a weekend breakfast or during a quiet evening at home. This shows respect for the importance of the conversation and ensures everyone can focus fully on it.

Another crucial aspect of these conversations is maintaining emotional balance. While it's natural to feel passionate about your career choices, getting defensive or angry can shut down productive dialogue. Instead, try using phrases like *"I understand your concern about..."* or *"I've thought about that, and here's my plan..."* This approach shows that you're taking their input seriously while still advocating for your own choices.

- Create a presentation or vision board about your career plans

- Share success stories of people in your chosen field

- Develop a backup plan to address financial or practical concerns

- Be open to compromise and alternative pathways

- Keep the conversation ongoing rather than trying to resolve everything at once

One effective technique I've found in my career guidance practice is the "bridge building" approach. This involves finding common ground between your aspirations and your parents' concerns. For example, if your parents value financial stability and you're interested in a creative field, you might discuss how you plan to combine your creative pursuits with practical business skills. This shows that you're thinking about both your passion and practical considerations.

Remember that these conversations are usually part of an ongoing dialogue rather than a one-time discussion. Be patient with the process and understand that your parents' perspective might evolve as they see you taking concrete steps toward your goals. Keep them updated on your progress, share your successes (even small ones), and be honest about your challenges.

- Document your career exploration journey to share with parents
- Set up meetings with professionals in your field of interest
- Consider job shadowing or internship opportunities
- Create a timeline of your career development plans
- Stay open to feedback and suggestions

Building trust through actions is just as important as communication. Show your commitment to your chosen path through consistent effort - whether that's maintaining good grades, pursuing relevant extracurricular activities, or gaining experience through part-time work or volunteering. When parents see you taking practical steps toward your goals, they're often more likely to support your choices.

If conversations become heated or unproductive, taking a step back is okay. You might say something like, *"I appreciate you sharing your thoughts. Could we take some time to think about this and continue our discussion later?"* This shows maturity and helps prevent damaging your relationship over career disagreements.

Remember that your parents' concerns often come from a place of care and experience. While they may not always express it perfectly, most parents want to protect their children from potential hardships and ensure their future success. By approaching these conversations with understanding, preparation, and patience, you can work toward finding common ground and building support for your career choices.

Managing Cultural and Generational Expectations in Career Choices

Cultural and generational expectations around career choices can feel like carrying a heavy backpack filled with everyone else's dreams and traditions. Whether you're from a family that values certain professions over others or you're navigating between traditional career paths and modern opportunities, finding your way requires both understanding and strategy.

In my career guidance practice, I worked with Raj, a tech-savvy 16-year-old who dreamed of becoming a digital content creator. His parents, both successful doctors, struggled to understand how making videos could be a "real career". Like many teens from immigrant families, Raj felt caught between his passion for digital media and his family's traditional definition of success. Through our sessions, we developed approaches to help him bridge this cultural and generational gap while staying true to his aspirations.

- Research and present modern career statistics and success stories
- Demonstrate how traditional values apply to modern careers
- Find ways to honor family traditions while pursuing personal goals
- Create a detailed plan showing the viability of your chosen path
- Build a support network of mentors who understand both perspectives

One effective strategy is to help parents see how modern careers often incorporate traditional values in new ways. For instance, if your family values education and helping others, you might show how creating educational content online can impact thousands of learners worldwide. Or, if your family emphasizes business success, demonstrate how digital skills and entrepreneurship align with those values.

Generational gaps in career understanding often stem from rapid technological and social changes. Your parents' generation might have valued job security and traditional professional paths, while you see opportunities in emerging fields they might not fully comprehend. The key is to help bridge this understanding gap through education and open dialogue.

- Share articles and resources about emerging career fields
- Connect traditional skills with modern applications
- Highlight successful professionals who bridge traditional and modern careers
- Show how your chosen path can provide stability and growth
- Demonstrate your practical approach to career planning

Cultural expectations can be particularly challenging when they conflict with your personal career aspirations. Remember that it's possible to respect your cultural heritage while pursuing contemporary career opportunities. Consider finding ways to integrate cultural values into your career plans rather than viewing them as opposing forces.

For example, if you come from a culture that values community service and are interested in technology, you might explore how tech skills can be used for social good or community development. This approach shows how modern career choices can align with traditional cultural values.

- Identify shared values between your goals and cultural traditions
- Look for ways to blend cultural strengths with modern opportunities
- Find role models who successfully navigate similar cultural dynamics
- Create opportunities for family to engage with your career interests
- Develop a career narrative that honors both tradition and innovation

Managing expectations also means being patient with the process. Your family's understanding and acceptance of your career choices may evolve gradually. Continue demonstrating your commitment through consistent effort and achievement in your chosen field. Share your successes, no matter how small, and show how you apply family values like hard work, dedication, and responsibility to your modern career path.

Remember that you're not alone in navigating these challenges. Many successful professionals have faced similar cultural and generational gaps in their career journeys. Consider seeking mentors who understand your cultural background and can help you bridge these differences while building a successful career path.

Most importantly, approach these discussions with empathy and understanding. Your parents' concerns often come from a place of care and experience, even if their perspective differs from yours. By showing how you can honor their values while pursuing your passions, you can work toward building mutual understanding and support for your career choices.

Building Self-Confidence: Overcoming Career-Related Self-Doubt and Imposter Syndrome

Have you ever felt like everyone else has it all figured out while you're just pretending to know what you're doing? That nagging feeling of self-doubt or the worry that you're not good enough to pursue your dream career is more common than you might think - especially among teenagers exploring their future paths.

In my career guidance practice, I worked with Lily, a brilliant 16-year-old who excelled in computer programming but constantly doubted her abilities. Despite winning several coding competitions, she often said, *"I just got lucky"*, or *"Anyone could have done it"*. This is a classic example of imposter syndrome - feeling like you're not as capable as others perceive you to be, even when evidence shows otherwise.

- Recognize that self-doubt is a normal part of growth
- Challenge negative self-talk with evidence of your achievements
- Keep a "wins journal" to document your successes
- Share your feelings with trusted friends or mentors
- Focus on progress rather than perfection

One of the most effective ways to build self-confidence is through what I call the "small wins strategy". Instead of focusing on big, overwhelming career goals, break them down into smaller, achievable steps. Each small success builds your confidence and provides evidence against self-doubt.

For example, if you're interested in writing, start with a personal blog rather than immediately trying to publish a book. If you're drawn to business, sell items online or start a small service in your neighborhood. These small steps create a foundation of real experience that can help combat imposter syndrome.

- Set realistic, achievable goals.
- Celebrate small victories along the way.
- Learn from setbacks without letting them define you

- Build a support network of peers and mentors
- Take on gradually increasing challenges

Another powerful technique for building confidence is what I call evidence-collecting. Write down every accomplishment - completing a project, receiving positive feedback, or learning a new skill - and review your evidence of success when self-doubt creeps in. This concrete proof of your capabilities can help counter feelings of inadequacy.

Remember that even experienced professionals sometimes experience imposter syndrome. The key is not to eliminate self-doubt completely (which isn't realistic) but to learn how to move forward despite it. Think of self-doubt like a backseat driver - you can acknowledge its presence without letting it take the wheel.

- Create a portfolio of your achievements
- Seek feedback from trusted mentors
- Practice positive self-talk
- Develop your skills through continuous learning
- Help others who are earlier in their journey

One particularly effective strategy I've found is the "future self" exercise. Imagine yourself five years from now, having achieved your career goals. What would that version of you say to your current self about the doubts you're experiencing? This perspective shift can help you see your current challenges as temporary stepping stones rather than permanent barriers.

It's also important to understand that making mistakes and facing setbacks is a normal part of any career journey. Instead of viewing these experiences as evidence of inadequacy, try to see them as valuable learning opportunities. Every successful person has faced failures along the way—what matters is how you respond to and grow from these experiences.

- View challenges as opportunities for growth
- Learn from mistakes rather than dwelling on them
- Seek out constructive feedback

- Build resilience through gradual exposure to challenges

- Maintain a growth mindset

Remember Lily? She kept a "coding wins" journal, documenting her achievements, positive feedback, and learning experiences through our work together. She also began mentoring younger students in coding, which helped her recognize how much knowledge she actually possessed. Today, she confidently pursues her tech career goals, still experiencing occasional self-doubt but not letting it hold her back.

Building self-confidence is like building muscle - it requires consistent effort and practice. Start with small challenges and gradually take on bigger ones. Celebrate your successes, learn from setbacks, and remember that feeling uncertain doesn't mean you're incapable. With time and practice, you'll develop the confidence to pursue your career goals, even when self-doubt tries to hold you back. As we wrap up this chapter on navigating family dynamics and building self-confidence in your career journey, remember that the path to your dream career isn't always straight - and that's totally okay! Throughout this chapter, we've explored how to have meaningful conversations with parents about your career choices, manage cultural and generational expectations, and build the confidence needed to pursue your dreams.

Maya's story of bridging the gap between her passion for environmental science and her family's medical tradition shows us that finding common ground with preparation, patience, and open dialogue is possible. Just like her, you can learn to present your career aspirations effectively while respecting family values and constructively addressing concerns.

We've also tackled the very real challenges of self-doubt and imposter syndrome. Remember Lily's journey from constantly doubting her coding abilities to confidently pursuing her tech career goals? Her experience reminds us that feeling uncertain doesn't mean you're incapable - it's often just part of the growth process.

The strategies we've covered - from the "research first, talk later" method to the "small wins strategy" and "evidence collecting" - are tools you can use repeatedly as you navigate your career path. These aren't just one-time solutions but ongoing practices that can help you build confidence and maintain healthy family relationships throughout your career journey.

Whether dealing with cultural expectations like Raj, managing generational gaps in understanding modern careers, or battling self-doubt like Lily, remember you're not alone. Many successful professionals have faced similar challenges and found ways to stay true to themselves while building bridges of understanding with their families.

Moving forward, try implementing some of the communication strategies we discussed in your next family conversation about careers. Start small - maybe start with that "wins journal", or take one step toward building evidence for your chosen career path. Remember, every successful career journey starts with small steps and grows through consistent effort.

Your career path is uniquely yours, but that doesn't mean you have to navigate it alone. By combining open communication with family, strategic planning, and continuous self-development, you can build a career that honors both your aspirations and your family's values while staying true to yourself.

As you move into the next chapter, carry with you the confidence that you can handle difficult career conversations and overcome self-doubt. Your voice matters, your dreams are valid, and with the right tools and support, you can build a career path that's authentically yours.

Chapter 10

Your Success Blueprint

Creating a Flexible Career Strategy

Creating a successful career strategy isn't about plotting an unchangeable course through life - it's about developing a flexible blueprint that can evolve with you and the changing world of work. Like an architect designing a building that can withstand different weather conditions, your career strategy needs to be both sturdy enough to support your goals and flexible enough to adapt to new opportunities and challenges. Just as an architect needs both creativity and technical skills to design buildings that stand the test of time, you'll need a combination of vision and practical planning to build a career that can weather life's changes. This chapter will guide you through creating your own success blueprint - a flexible career strategy that grows and adapts with you.

Think of your career journey as a road trip. While it's good to have a destination in mind, the most memorable adventures often come from being open to unexpected detours and discovering new paths along the way. Your success blueprint isn't about creating a rigid, unchangeable plan - it's about developing a framework that helps you make informed decisions while staying adaptable to new opportunities.

In my career guidance practice, I worked with Jordan, a focused 18-year-old who had meticulously planned every step of his future tech career. His plan was rigid: graduate with a computer science degree, join a major tech company and climb the corporate ladder. However, we discussed the importance of building flexibility into his career strategy during our sessions. Together, we created a more adaptable plan that included multiple pathways to success. When the tech industry experienced unexpected shifts during his first year of college, Jordan's flexible strategy allowed him to pivot smoothly. While tutoring classmates, he discovered a passion for tech education and added teaching certification courses to his studies. Today, he successfully combines software development work with creating coding education content, a career combination he hadn't initially imagined. His story illustrates how a flexible career strategy can turn unexpected changes into opportunities for growth and fulfillment.

Creating your success blueprint isn't about predicting the future but preparing for it. In this chapter, we'll explore how to build a career strategy that's both sturdy enough to support your goals and flexible enough to embrace new opportunities. You'll learn how to identify potential pivot points in your career journey, develop backup plans that feel empowering rather than limiting, and set meaningful milestones that keep you moving forward while maintaining the freedom to adjust your course.

By the end of this chapter, you'll have the tools to create your own adaptable career strategy that honors your current dreams while leaving room for the amazing possibilities you haven't even discovered yet. Remember, the most successful careers often look very different from their original blueprints, and that's not just okay - it's often what makes them extraordinary.

Strategic Planning: Creating Your Five-Year Flexible Career Map

Let's dive into creating your five-year career map. Think of it as your personal GPS for success, but way cooler because you get to program all the destinations! While five years might seem like forever (I mean, that's like waiting for five new iPhone releases), having a flexible roadmap helps you stay focused while keeping your options open for awesome detours along the way.

Here are the key elements your five-year map should include:

- Your current starting point (skills, interests, education level)

- Major milestones you want to hit (think education goals, skill certifications, work experience)

- Potential pivot points where you might want to explore different paths

- Backup routes for when life throws those unexpected curveballs

- Resources you'll need along the way (mentors, training, networking opportunities)

Creating your map isn't about locking yourself into one path - it's about having a general direction while staying open to cool opportunities that pop up along the way. Think of it like planning a road trip: You know your destination, but you're totally open to checking out that amazing ice cream shop someone recommended or that cool scenic route you discovered.

I remember working with Kai, a student who loved both coding and music. Instead of choosing just one path, we created a flexible five-year map with multiple routes. His primary path focused on software development, with checkpoints for learning specific programming languages and building his portfolio. However, we also included parallel tracks for music production and sound engineering, creating opportunities for these interests to intersect. Today, Kai develops audio software for music producers - a career he hadn't even known existed when he started planning.

When mapping out your five-year plan, break it down into smaller chunks that feel less overwhelming. Start by detailing your first year, then create broader strokes for years 2-5.

Here's how to structure it:

- Year 1: Set specific, detailed quarterly goals

- Years 2-3: Create broader six-month milestone targets

- Years 4-5: Outline general directions and major goals

- Review and adjust every 3-6 months

Remember, your career map isn't written in stone - it's more like a Google Map that recalculates when you take an unexpected turn. The key is to stay flexible while keeping your ultimate goals in sight. Maybe you start out wanting to be a graphic designer but discover you love the business side of creative work even more. That's not a detour - it's an upgrade to your route!

One of the most powerful aspects of a five-year map is identifying potential pivot points - those moments where you might want to shift direction based on new opportunities or interests. These could be after completing a certification, finishing a major project, or gaining specific experience in your field. Having these pivot points clearly marked helps you stay alert to new possibilities while maintaining momentum toward your goals.

Think about building regular check-in points to assess your progress and make adjustments.

These "recalculation stops" might include:

- Quarterly reviews of your short-term goals
- Annual assessments of your overall direction
- Skill inventory updates every six months
- Network expansion check-ins every few months

Your five-year map should also include what I call "skill stacking" - planning how different abilities can combine to create unique career opportunities. For instance, if you're interested in social media marketing, you might stack skills like content creation, basic design, analytics, and trend forecasting. Each skill builds on the others, creating more possibilities for your future.

The most successful career maps include both professional and personal development goals. While planning those career milestones, don't forget to include goals for developing soft skills like communication, leadership, and adaptability. These skills are like the suspension system in your career vehicle - they help you smoothly handle any bumps in the road.

Remember, the goal isn't to predict your future perfectly - it's to create a flexible framework that helps you make informed decisions while staying open to amazing possibilities you haven't even imagined yet. Your five-year map is a living document that grows and evolves with you, helping you navigate toward success while embracing the exciting twists and turns along the way.

Identifying Pivot Points: Building Career Adaptability and Backup Plans

Ever feel like you're playing a video game where the rules keep changing? That's what career planning is like these days! Just as gamers need multiple save points and power-ups to succeed, you need pivot points and backup plans in your career journey. Let's talk about how to build these into your strategy while keeping things flexible and fun.

Pivot points are like those moments in a game where you can choose different paths - they're opportunities to shift direction based on new information or changing circumstances. Think of them as strategic checkpoints to assess your progress and decide if you want to continue on your current path or explore a new direction.

Here are some key moments that often serve as natural pivot points:

- After completing a certification or training program
- When finishing an internship or major project
- During significant industry changes
- When new technologies create fresh opportunities
- After gaining specific experience or skills

I recently worked with Tara, a student who initially planned to become a traditional graphic designer. She wisely built several pivot points into her career strategy. After completing her first design certification, she discovered the growing UX/UI design field. Because she had identified this moment as a potential pivot point, she was ready to explore this new direction while still building on her existing skills. Today, she combines both traditional graphic design and UX work, creating a unique career path she loves.

Building career adaptability is like developing your character's skills in a game - the more versatile you are, the better equipped you'll be to handle different challenges.

Here's how to level up your career adaptability:

- Learn transferable skills that work across multiple industries
- Stay current with industry trends and technological changes
- Build a strong professional network that spans different fields
- Maintain an emergency fund for transition periods
- Keep your skills portfolio updated and diverse

Creating backup plans isn't about expecting failure - it's about being smart and prepared. Think of them as your career cheat codes (except they're totally legal!). Your backup plans should be exciting alternatives you'd genuinely enjoy pursuing, not just last-resort options.

When developing your backup plans, consider these strategies:

- Identify parallel careers that use similar skills

- Explore related fields where your experience would be valuable
- Consider how your hobbies could become income streams
- Look for ways to combine different interests into unique opportunities
- Keep your skills updated in multiple areas

One effective way to build adaptability is through what I call the "Skills Triangle" approach. Instead of focusing on just one area, develop skills in three related but different areas. For example, if you're interested in social media marketing, you might develop skills in content creation, data analytics, and graphic design. This way, you have multiple directions you can pivot toward while maintaining a cohesive professional story.

Remember that career adaptability isn't just about having technical skills—it's also about developing your emotional resilience and adaptability mindset. Practice being comfortable with change by regularly taking on new challenges, even small ones. For example, you could try learning a new app, taking on a different responsibility at your part-time job, or volunteering in a role that stretches your comfort zone.

I worked with Miguel, who taught me a valuable lesson about backup plans. While pursuing his main interest in environmental science, he maintained his skills in digital content creation through a YouTube channel about environmental issues. When funding for environmental research became tight in his area, he smoothly transitioned to environmental education and content creation while continuing to build his expertise. His backup plan wasn't just a safety net - it became a unique way to pursue his passion from a different angle.

Think of your career journey as a choose-your-own-adventure story. Each pivot point is a new chapter in which you make choices that shape your path. The key is to stay flexible, keep learning, and remember that changing direction isn't a setback—it's often the beginning of an even better adventure.

By building in pivot points, developing adaptability, and creating exciting backup plans, you're not just preparing for the future but creating multiple paths to success. Remember, the most interesting careers often come from being ready to say "yes" to unexpected opportunities while having the skills and preparation to make the most of them.

Goal Setting and Milestone Creation: From Vision to Action Steps

Let's talk about turning those big career dreams into actual reality - because having fantastic goals is great, but knowing how to reach them? That's where the real magic happens! Think of your career goals like building an epic playlist - you need both those amazing headliners (your big vision) and those perfect transitions (your milestones) to make it flow just right.

I remember working with Zoe, a student who felt totally overwhelmed by her dream of becoming a digital content creator. She had this amazing vision but didn't know where to start. Together, we broke down her big goal into smaller, achievable steps - like creating a staircase to her dreams instead of facing a giant wall.

Here are the key elements for turning your vision into action:

- Break big goals into smaller, 90-day chunks
- Create specific, measurable action steps
- Set both skill-based and experience-based milestones
- Include learning goals and networking targets
- Build in regular progress check-ins

The secret to effective goal setting is making your goals SMART (Specific, Measurable, Achievable, Relevant, and Time-bound). Instead of saying, *"I want to work in tech"*, try something like, *"I will complete a basic coding certification in Python within the next three months"*.

When creating your milestones, think about them as levels in a video game. Each level builds on the skills and achievements from the previous one, gradually leading you toward your ultimate goal.

For instance, if your dream is to become a social media manager, your **milestone progression might look like this:**

- Level 1: Create and grow your own social media presence
- Level 2: Volunteer to manage social media for a school club or local nonprofit
- Level 3: Complete a social media marketing certification

- Level 4: Land your first paid client or internship
- Level 5: Build a portfolio of successful campaigns

One of the most powerful techniques I've found is what I call the "Success Ladder" approach. Start by visualizing your end goal, then work backward to create a series of increasingly challenging but achievable steps. Each step should be significant enough to feel like real progress but small enough to accomplish within a reasonable timeframe.

For example, when working with Marcus, who dreamed of starting his own web design business, **we created a Success Ladder that looked like this:**

- Learn basic HTML and CSS (3 months)
- Build personal portfolio website (1 month)
- Create free websites for three local nonprofits (4 months)
- Take a business basics course (2 months)
- Land first paying client (2 months)
- Scale to three regular clients (6 months)

Remember to celebrate your wins along the way - even the small ones! Each milestone you reach proves that you're moving in the right direction. Keep a progress journal or create a visual tracker to help you see how far you've come. It's like having your own career achievement board!

Here's a pro tip: Build in what I call "flexibility checkpoints" - regular moments to assess and adjust your goals based on new opportunities or changing interests. Maybe you discover a new aspect of your field that excites you, or perhaps technology creates a new career path you haven't considered. Your goals should be firm enough to keep you motivated but flexible enough to evolve with you.

When setting your milestones, consider these different types:

- Skill milestones (learning specific abilities)
- Experience milestones (gaining practical knowledge)
- Network milestones (building professional connections)

- Portfolio milestones (creating tangible work examples)
- Personal development milestones (growing soft skills)

Don't forget to make your goals visible! Whether you have a vision board on your wall, a detailed plan on your phone, or regular reminders in your calendar, keeping your goals and milestones in sight helps maintain your motivation and focus.

Remember, the path to your dreams isn't always straight. Sometimes, you'll need to adjust your milestones or even revise your primary goals - and that's totally okay! What matters is maintaining forward momentum while staying true to your values and interests.

As you work through your milestones, keep track of what you learn along the way. Each experience, whether it goes according to plan or not, teaches you something valuable about yourself and your chosen path. These insights can help you refine your goals and create even better action steps for the future.

Your career journey is uniquely yours, and your goals should reflect that. Don't feel pressured to set milestones that match someone else's timeline or expectations. Focus on creating goals that challenge you while remaining achievable and authentic to who you are and who you want to become.

As we wrap up this chapter on creating your success blueprint, remember that the most successful career journeys often look nothing like their original plans - and that's exactly what makes them amazing! Your career strategy isn't meant to be a rigid roadmap but a flexible framework that grows and evolves with you.

Think back to Jordan's story - how his willingness to adapt his tech career plans led him to discover an unexpected passion for teaching that enhanced his journey rather than derailing it. Your career path might take similar surprising turns, and that's totally okay! In fact, it's these unexpected twists that often lead to the most fulfilling opportunities.

Throughout this chapter, we've explored how to create a five-year flexible career map, identify strategic pivot points, and set meaningful milestones.

Key Takeaways

The key takeaway? Success isn't about sticking to one unchangeable plan - it's about staying adaptable while keeping your core goals in sight. Whether you're mapping out your education path, planning your skill development, or creating backup plans, remember that flexibility is your superpower.

As you move forward with your own career planning, **keep these essential strategies in mind:**

- Create goals that excite you while leaving room for unexpected opportunities

- Build in regular checkpoints to assess and adjust your plans

- Develop multiple skills that can be combined in unique ways

- Stay open to new possibilities while maintaining momentum toward your goals

- Celebrate your progress, even the small wins

Your career journey is uniquely yours, and there's no one "right" way to pursue your dreams. The strategies and tools we've discussed are like different apps on your phone - use the ones that work best for you and customize them to fit your needs. Some days, you'll follow your plan exactly, and other days, you'll need to recalculate your route - both are perfectly fine!

Remember, every successful career story includes plot twists, character development, and surprising discoveries along the way. Your job isn't to predict every step of your journey perfectly - it's to create a flexible framework that helps you make informed decisions while staying open to amazing possibilities you haven't even imagined yet.

As you close this chapter and continue building your own success blueprint, trust that you have the tools and adaptability to handle whatever challenges and opportunities come your way. Your future is bright, and the best part? You get to be the architect of your own success story.

Now it's your turn to take these strategies and make them your own. Start small, dream big, and remember that every step forward - even in an unexpected direction - is progress toward your goals. Your career journey is just beginning, and with your flexible success blueprint in hand, you're ready to take on whatever incredible opportunities come your way!

Leave A Review

Thank You!

If this book resonated with you or supported you in any way, you're warmly invited to leave a **review** on the platform where you purchased this book — reviews help other readers discover books like this.

If you'd like, you can also access an **optional companion resource** created to support and complement your reading experience.

Scan Me: REVIEW and download optional COMPANION RESOURCE

Conclusion

As we reach the end of our journey together, I want you to remember something crucial: your career path is uniquely yours. Throughout this book, we've explored numerous stories of teens who faced challenges similar to yours - from Sarah finding a way to combine art and medicine to Emma building her experience bank from scratch to Jordan creating a flexible career strategy that allowed him to adapt and thrive.

The world of work is evolving faster than ever before, presenting both challenges and incredible opportunities. You've learned the importance of understanding your Career DNA through the Ikigai framework, explored the possibilities of portfolio careers, and discovered how to leverage AI and technology to create your own opportunities. You now have the tools to build a strong personal brand, navigate family expectations, and create multiple income streams that align with your passions.

Remember that feeling overwhelmed or uncertain about your future is completely normal. What matters is how you channel that energy into positive action. Use the strategies we've discussed - whether it's building your experience bank, creating a flexible career blueprint, or exploring alternative education paths - to take small steps forward each day. Your career journey isn't about making one perfect choice; it's about making informed decisions that you can adjust as you grow and opportunities emerge.

Keep in mind that success looks different for everyone. Some of you might choose traditional career paths, others might become entrepreneurs, and many might create unique combinations of both. What's important is that you stay true to your values while remaining adaptable to change. The skills you've learned in this book - from financial literacy to personal branding, networking to family communication - will serve you well regardless of your specific path.

Most importantly, remember that you're not alone on this journey. The stories shared throughout this book demonstrate that many others have faced and overcome similar challenges. Whether dealing with parental pressure like Maya, exploring multiple passions like Olivia, or searching for ways to fund your education like Mia, solutions and support are always available.

As you step forward into your career journey, carry the confidence that comes from being prepared. You have the tools to create a future that's both professionally fulfilling and personally meaningful. Your career path may not be straight, and that's okay - some of the most rewarding journeys involve unexpected turns and discoveries.

Trust in your ability to adapt and grow. Embrace the opportunities that come your way, learn from the challenges you face, and keep building your skills and experiences. Whether heading to college or trade school, starting a business, or exploring alternative paths, remember that your future is truly in your hands. You have the power to shape it in ways that align with your values, interests, and aspirations.

The end of this book is really just the beginning of your journey. Take what you've learned here and use it as a foundation to build your unique path forward. Your future is waiting, and you're well-equipped to make it extraordinary. Keep learning, stay curious, and never be afraid to adjust your course as you grow. Your career journey is a marathon, not a sprint, and every step you take brings you closer to creating a future that's authentically yours.

Bibliography

Based on the content of this career guidance book, here is a bibliography of relevant sources:

Duckworth, A. (2016). Grit: The Power of Passion and Perseverance. Scribner.

Gladwell, M. (2008). Outliers: The Story of Success. Little, Brown and Company.

Ibarra, H. (2003). Working Identity: Unconventional Strategies for Reinventing Your Career. Harvard Business School Press.

Kiyosaki, R. (2017). Why A Students Work for C Students and B Students Work for the Government. Plata Publishing.

Newport, C. (2012). So Good They Can't Ignore You: Why Skills Trump Passion in the Quest for Work You Love. Grand Central Publishing.

Robinson, K. (2009). The Element: How Finding Your Passion Changes Everything. Penguin Books.

Sinek, S. (2009). Start with Why: How Great Leaders Inspire Everyone to Take Action.

Yoshinori, M. & García, H. (2017). Ikigai: The Japanese Secret to a Long and Happy Life. Penguin Life.